Viral
marketing

RUSSELL GOLDSMITH

Viral
marketing

Get your audience to do
your marketing for you

An imprint of Pearson Education

London • New York • Toronto • Sydney • Tokyo • Singapore • Hong Kong • Cape Town

New Delhi • Madrid • Paris • Amsterdam • Munich • Milan • Stockholm

PEARSON EDUCATION LIMITED

Head Office:
Edinburgh Gate
Harlow CM20 2JE
Tel: +44 (0)1279 623623
Fax: +44 (0)1279 431059

London Office:
128 Long Acre
London WC2E 9AN
Tel: +44 (0)20 7447 2000
Fax: +44 (0)20 7447 2170

_____

First published in Great Britain in 2002

© Pearson Education Limited 2002

The right of Russell Goldsmith to be identified as Author
of this Work has been asserted by him in accordance
with the Copyright, Designs and Patents Act 1988.

ISBN 0273 65905 7

British Library Cataloguing in Publication Data
A CIP catalogue record for this book can be obtained from the British Library

Library of Congress Cataloging in Publication Data Applied for.

10 9 8 7 6 5 4 3 2 1

Designed by Claire Brodmann Book Designs, Lichfield, Staffs
Typeset by Northern Phototypesetting Co. Ltd, Bolton
Printed and bound in Great Britain by Bell & Bain Ltd, Glasgow

The Publishers' policy is to use paper manufactured from sustainable forests.

Foreword

The internet has demonstrated that we are social animals. Far from isolating people, this technology has brought us together. In particular, email makes it easier to stay in touch, talk and yes even gossip. Indeed, this is why viral marketing works as it uses our fundamental interest in being part of a larger group of friends or network of people. Understanding this social change is a pre-requisite for all those who are interested in mass communication. This is a new mechanism to talk and listen to customers. It is early days yet, but this book neatly encapsulates some of the insights so far.

Many popular commentators spend their time wringing their hands as to the negative impact of new technology. Part of the argument is that we are losing our sense of community and our roots. We do not have time for our children, friends or relatives. They hark back to the days when we lived in small villages or communities when we all knew one another and could chat about the new issues.

A more constructive view of technology is that it has enabled us all to participate in the best pieces of previous better days; but more efficiently or productively. For communication, internet based email has massively expanded our potential to talk and entertain one another. Quicker than letters, less

obtrusive than phone calls, email can be our own method to broadcast interesting ideas and news, especially as we move apart from school friends, work colleagues and local communities.

The traffic of ideas and personal news on the internet is the product of our desire for social interaction. Obviously it is just like word of mouth of old, but differs in the scope and scale by which messages can be communicated. The ripple of a cool idea, joke or just straight news can be so quick and extensive because of the ease of passing email to those who are interested.

It is surprising, that the internet as a media for the exchange of ideas has not attracted more attention from those interested in mass communication. Perhaps this is because it is fundamentally different from broadcasting as it is interactive, hard to edit and seems to have a life of it's own. Nonetheless this book shows how powerful this medium can be.

Perhaps the best recommendation for more attention to viral marketing is that customers really like it when done well. Simply, it makes life easier and more interesting.

John Browett
CEO of tesco.com

Acknowledgments

There are quite a few people I need to thank, mainly for putting up with me while writing this book. First, to my wife, Ruth, and children, Tara and Daniel, who have been patient with my disappearing to the study every weekend as well as spending half our summer holiday researching on the internet. To all those friends who didn't take the proverbial when I told them I was writing a book, but instead encouraged me by pointing me in various directions with my research, especially Terry and Nik. To all those at Markettiers4dc Limited, the Clerkenwell-based marketing company I am a director of, who have shown an interest in my writing. My thanks go especially to my fellow directors, Howard, Karen, Oliver, Marcel and Nik, who have had the confidence in me that I would not lose focus on the task in hand of growing our business while at the same time concentrating on my writing. To all those who have helped contribute to the book, from taking part in my survey through to offering or agreeing to be interviewed. I would especially like to thank Dave Gorman who, as part of his interview, answered questions over email in between shows on Broadway in New York! And finally, to Rachael, Rachel, Ellie, Adam and Angela and everyone at Prentice Hall Business for offering me this opportunity.

Contents

Introduction

There are certain things in life that I find quite amazing. Granted, small coincidences of this kind don't quite match up to the Seven Wonders of the World, but in my little world it was quite significant and relevant to my book. I decided to write this book while on holiday with my family and some friends in Delray Beach, Florida; a long way from the day-to-day dramas of my job in Clerkenwell, London, where, from 7.30am when I arrive at work, until I pack up and head for home, my day tends to be dictated by what arrives in my in-tray. However, like a lot of people today, this is no longer a physical in-tray of memos, letters and faxes, but the virtual in-tray in my Microsoft Outlook folder. This is an in-tray that, when an email arrives, causes my colleague who had just sent it and who sits no more than three metres away to shout across and say: 'Russ. I've just sent you an email. It's about a meeting we're going to in an hour. I'll talk you through it in the cab, but basically, what it said was. . .' What is it about office culture today that we now have to communicate digitally, only then to reiterate whatever it was that we sent, by explaining it all face to face as we would have done before?

Anyway, what was amazing? Well, the reason I wanted to write the book on holiday was that I thought my mind would be free of everything related to email and marketing while I was away (and therefore more objective and less cluttered). Yet literally the evening I sat down to start this introduction, my friend turned around and said: 'Have you heard about FriendsReunited?[1] It's the most incredible website.' 'Actually', I replied, 'I registered a couple of weeks ago and I've already been in touch with two mates who I hadn't spoken to for at least 17 years. I've told loads of people about it.' My friend's husband then decides to check his email and turns to his wife and says: 'How weird, you have got an email from that FriendsReunited you were just talking about – someone from your school has registered! Do you want to check it out?'

And there you have it. The introduction to my book was complete. Here I was, after months of preparation, ready to start with a theoretically based 'where did it all start, who was the first, what it all meant' etc., but the perfect introduction was formed in the final conversation before I switched on my laptop. Here is a website that has spent exactly nothing on marketing, yet, at the time of writing, was receiving new registrations at a phenomenal rate. While on holiday, the most up-to-date statistic I had on this particular website was that it was increasing members at a rate of 10,000 to 15,000 per day and had around 800,000 registered users.[2] Yet, within a couple of months, that number had increased to 25,000 new users per day, with the number of registered users totalling 2.3 million.[3] And what was all the fuss about with this UK-based internet phenomenon? Basically, it is a database of all the schools in the UK (past and present), which allows you to register for free under the school you attended, making a note of the year you left, together with a few notes on what you're up to with some contact details. It was set up by Steve Pankhurst after his wife had come up with the idea while she was pregnant, when she wondered what her old friends were doing at the time. After looking on the web and only finding

message boards for people to post to, looking for other people, Steve thought it would be simple to create something that was easy to use, based around the school that people studied at rather than the person.[4]

FriendsReunited is a site that everyone I know is talking about and it's the perfect example of how something can be marketed virally, whether intentionally or not! I received an email from my brother, who attended the same school as me, telling me to check out the site and register. When I did, I saw names of pupils listed that I knew and immediately contacted them by email. I also registered for updates from the site when people from my school joined and so far I have received numerous email updates that allow me to click on a link to direct me back to the appropriate part of the site for me. I then recommended it to friends via email. No wonder it's a success – if just a small percentage of its user base is passing its address on as actively as I am, then it will grow immensely! Pankhurst believes its success lies in the fact that it affects everyone as we are all interested and nosey enough to want to know what our former classmates are doing now.[5] Oh, and here I am mentioning it in the first pages of my book for hopefully a few more thousand people to hear about it!

FriendsReunited is a site that everyone I know is talking about.

So there you have it, viral marketing explained. Well, perhaps there's a little more to it than that and hopefully this book will explain what it is about viral marketing that has encouraged it out of the New Media clique and into mainstream advertising and PR functions.

In the first chapter, I outline what viral marketing is all about, explaining how it has evolved from traditional 'word-of-mouth' marketing to offer opportunities to companies to spread their messages faster than they could ever have imagined a few years ago. I will show, however, that, as with word of mouth, you are at the mercy of your customers and, therefore, just as viral marketing can work wonders for a brand, it can work against one too. Finally, an introduction to the concept would not be complete without giving someone credit for starting it all off. I therefore complete the chapter by outlining a very early example of a campaign that was called at the time a 'media virus', followed with a discussion on the company that is acknowledged within the industry to have been the first to implement a truly viral marketing campaign.

Chapter 2 starts by looking at our communication patterns, the way we connect with other people and how we have a desire to be part of a group. I investigate how people's attitudes can be influenced by certain individuals and report on the work carried out by Burson-Marsteller in the USA, who highlighted the people within the online population who can make or break a product or service's success. I then look at why certain ideas will be passed from one person to another, briefly discussing the concept of memetics, first introduced by Richard Dawkins. Here we look at the transfer of replicating units that make a recipient alter his own behaviour through replication or imitation, thereby passing on the meme to a further individual. This leads us on to Seth Godin's 'ideaviruses' and the fact that email has become so important in transferring information quickly and sometimes even instantly. This chapter will then look into understanding what motivates people into passing on a message to one or more people, with particular reference to groups of like-minded individuals and how important it is also to understand what subjects are taboo.

Chapter 3 furthers the investigation into why people pass on emails and SMS messages outlining findings of a survey commissioned exclusively for this book. The survey was carried out using online research site Tickbox.net, which has thousands of people subscribed to its mailing list, people ready and willing to participate in incentivized surveys. The survey was also publicized to the Pearson Publishing email mailing list and, of course, I wouldn't be doing my book justice if I had not included a link to it at the bottom of my email signature file for the duration of its availability. The chapter initially looks at how kids and teenagers have grown up in a world where email is just part of their everyday life. From a marketing point of view, however, there are a number of issues to consider if targeting this age group via such a medium is your objective. I have therefore outlined these by summarizing an interview I carried out with a representative of Cartoon Network, who comes across such issues on a daily basis. I then take a brief look at where it all started as far as email is concerned before discussing the types of email people receive today. My research then looks at whether or not people could live without email and SMS. I ask how they contact their friends the most, whether or not they open attached files or follow links to websites from emails and whether or not they have ever forwarded emails or SMS messages to friends or work colleagues. Finally, I investigate what would make them view and pass on attachments or links in emails. The survey also asked participants to tell me of a favourite email or SMS message they had received from a friend or work colleague that they then passed on to someone else.

Chapter 4 provides some excellent case studies showing how different strategies using varying methods of delivery can still achieve success for a viral marketing campaign. These examples outline the fact that there is no one specific method that should be followed. The first of these case studies comes from Australia, where an online retailer actually filmed a TV-style advert specifically for distribution over the web. The second example shows how incentives, including freebie giveaways, will help drive a viral campaign. Our third case study is really an opinion piece of my own and it describes how viral marketing can be used as a brand awareness exercise rather than be implemented as a means to drive traffic to a website or to grow a database. The fourth case study brings to our attention technologies from the USA, where video is embedded into an email without the need for plug-ins and where you are able to monitor every action that a user makes, whether viewing the email, or forwarding the message to a friend – scary! Our fifth example shows how viral marketing has already worked its way onto SMS and the chapter ends with a few examples of some campaigns that, in certain people's eyes, didn't quite come up to scratch.

In the final chapter, I discuss whether or not there really is a science to viral marketing. Can we really create a winning formula to work every time? I start by **Can we really create a** detailing some research from the USA on **winning formula to** top organizations' attitudes to viral cam- **work every time?** paigns and whether or not they will be implementing such a mechanic. Finally, I complete the book with information on how to maximize the success of a viral marketing campaign by carrying out a checklist of 20 key points. But I urge you, read the whole book first before sneaking to the end to find the answers – would you do that to any other decent mystery story?

What's it all about?

- Ownership and opportunities
- Threats
- Beginnings
- Key points and top tips

Ownership and opportunities

There is a misconception about a lot of New Media marketing that it's all something new and it requires 'New Media strategic experts' to handle it. But it shouldn't. The internet, interactive TV, wireless devices, these are all simply new channels for reaching a target audience, be they consumers or businesses. Therefore, the principles behind the thinking should always be the same. Granted, there is a need to understand the capabilities of the technologies that we now live and breathe everyday of our lives. Who knows where we would be without our email, our mobile phone, our PalmPilot or our reality TV show updates such as 'Big Brother' on digital TV with split-screen interactive viewing and onscreen voting. But the basics are the same. As consumers or business people, from the minute we wake up to the moment we fall asleep, we have a media diet that means we consume marketing messages all day through our radios, TV, newspapers and magazines, outdoor posters, websites, mobile phones and PDAs and, of course, through our email. The skill, for you, the marketer, is to understand who the target audience is, where to find them, what the right message is that will turn them on

1

yet relates to what they have to say and then knowing what mechanic will allow you to deliver it.

Viral marketing, however, provides us with an additional and arguably even greater challenge. How to then get that individual from the target audience to pass your message on to someone of similar mind and interest, thereby doing your marketing for you, through their own network of contacts. This is the challenge I will seek to answer in this book by explaining what the ingredients are to one simple email that can convert it from just another campaign into a massive marketing success.

Viral marketing, provides us with an additional and arguably even greater challenge.

As marketers, there is a battle over who 'owns' a viral marketing project. Brand and product managers can have a large number of marketing agencies working for them at any one time. With the marketing budget in general being made to stretch further and further with each passing quarter, there is a growing pressure for each of these agencies to remain creative and at the cutting edge. Coupled with this is the internal pressure at a company for someone in the marketing team also continually to show initiative, not to mention cost effectiveness and a decent return on investment. It is therefore no surprise, given that viral marketing is one of the new marketing buzzwords, that everyone involved is jumping on the viral marketing bandwagon.

The PR agency will say they should own it as you are not paying a media owner to run it, but the advertising agency will say it's in their domain as in some cases is it closer to creating an advertising or promotional campaign than it is a PR story. The New Media agency will scream for control as it will no doubt be designed using the latest web technologies and often link back to a website for data collection. And internally, the

IT team will probably shout that if all you are doing is sending out a bunch of emails, why the hell are you are paying someone to handle it externally?

So, is viral marketing nothing new then?

Well, not really no! It's simply word-of-mouth marketing via a digital platform, be that email, SMS or whatever new digital technology you are using to communicate with friends, family or work colleagues by the time you read this, the main difference being it can spread, across the world, both instantly and exponentially.[1]

Have you have ever liked something so much or found it so relevant to your work that you passed it on to a friend or colleague by email because you thought they would also like it or find it interesting? If you have, then congratulations – you too have been a part of the viral marketing experience.

In fact, to highlight the fact that it's nothing new, here is an example of what I believe is a traditional word-of-mouth story that has worked hand in hand with a viral aspect. Later in the book I will explain how this can be transformed into marketing campaigns.

An English comedian called Dave Gorman, in response to a bet with his flatmate, set out to find 54 other people called Dave Gorman, take a photograph of them, get them to sign it and shake their hand. His adventure took him across the world, forming a unique and highly entertaining one-man stand-up show and extremely enjoyable book (Gorman, D. and Wallace, D. (2001), Ebury Press *Are You Dave Gorman?*), as he and his flatmate describe how, after travelling over 25,000 miles, he eventually succeeded in his challenge! Again, this is a story that a friend told me and, wherever I went, people started discussing whether or not they actually knew someone called Dave Gorman. As it turns out, one of the suppliers to

my wife's food manufacturing company is actually called David Gorman!

So why mention this in my book as an example of how something that can spread virally can lead to success? Well, the comedian Dave Gorman, (as opposed to the supplier to my wife's company or, indeed any of the others) set up an email account so that anyone who was either called that name himself or knew someone with that name could get in touch. According to Gorman, email was 'essential' in helping his search. 'For me personally', he said, 'it allows a lot of contact with people without them knowing where I live! I can put my email address out into the world and get a lot of replies. They don't wake me up at 3am which would inevitably happen if my phone number was out there and I don't get strangers visiting my home.'[2] Incredibly enough, and much to his astonishment, a short time into his search, he started to receive emails from people he had never met providing him with leads as to where to find other people with the same name as his. At one point in his search, while doing his stage show in Edinburgh, he started getting up to 100 emails a day and when his TV show was aired, even though his search was complete, he started getting 400 emails a day. People had passed on his email address via emails to their friends around the world. 'I get sent copies of them sometimes where I'm added to the list and I can see that it's been sent to somebody's entire address book. Often hundreds of people.'[3] Some of the emails he received had been forwarded at least 20 times.[4] Without email and people passing the message virally, it could have taken him years to meet his challenge. Instead, he achieved it in a matter of months and was able to write an award-winning comedy show out of his story! And why did people help in his task? He's still not sure! But Gorman feels that the reason people pass on messages and jokes to their friends is that it's

just so easy and unobtrusive. He believes that emails 'don't disturb your day. They are a one-way communication so you don't have to hear about Gerald's hernia operation and how the kids are doing. You can just make your point.'[5]

There is no doubting that word of mouth forms an important part of the buying process, whether consumer or business to business. For example, as Emanuel Rosen points out:

- 65% of customers who bought a PalmPilot told the makers of this device that they had heard about it from another person.
- Friends and relatives are the number one source for information about places to visit or about flights, hotels or rental cars, according to the Travel Industry Association.
- 52% of moviegoers rely to some extent on a recommendation from someone they know, according to a study by Maritz Marketing Research, with 70% of Americans relying on the advice of others when selecting a new doctor, according to the same study.[6]

Rosen comments that most of today's marketing still focuses on how to use advertising and other tools to influence each customer individually, ignoring the fact that purchasing many types of product is part of a social process. He explains that it involves not only a one-to-one interaction between the company and the customer but also many exchanges of information and influence among the people who surround that customer.[7]

Viral marketing now has its place firmly set within the marketing mix.

So with the establishment of the fact that people are now passing on the word of mouth via their email, viral marketing now has its place firmly set within the marketing mix.

Threats

Just as a viral campaign can work for a brand, it can just as easily work against one too. As highlighted by IMT Strategies, the cost of overnight market coverage is a near total loss of control over the company's marketing message and brand as eager consumers indiscriminately 'spam'.[8]

The internet has also been an amazing leveller when it comes to giving small businesses the chance to compete with the 'big boys' or consumer action groups to fight against their commercial foes. With no high street presence required, a website can make any sole trader appear to be as big as a multinational organization. And even easier is the fact that anyone can send an email to find it is soon passed from desktop to desktop. An example of this is something that arrived in my in-tray in February 2001, passed on from a colleague in the office, who, incidentally, sent it to the other 40 or so people that work with me, outlining how quickly emails can spread virally. This story even found its way into national media, featured on the *Guardian*'s website on 19 February of that year. Whether the original emails in this documented email conversation are genuine or not, the fact is that this viral email is potentially extremely damaging to Niké, the company referred to throughout. The email arrived with the subject, 'The power of branding'. As is the nature of an email that has been passed on virally, there were a number of emails that said, 'you must read this' and such like, including email addresses of all those who had passed the original emails on. These have been deleted for the purpose of this book.

Subject: The power of branding
Date: Tue, 20 Feb 2001 07:22:34—0500
Nike now lets you personalize your shoes by
submitting a word or phrase which they will stitch
onto your shoes, under the swoosh. So Jonah Peretti
filled out the form and sent them $50 to stitch
"SWEATSHOP" onto his shoes.

Here's the responses he got...

* *
From: "Personalize, NIKE iD" <nikeid_personalize@nike.com
To: "'Jonah H. Peretti'"
Subject: RE: Your NIKE iD order o16468000

Your NIKE iD order was canceled for one or more of
the following reasons:

1. Your Personal iD contains another party's
   trademark or other intellectual property
2. Your Personal iD contains the name of an athlete
   or team we do not have the legal right to use
3. Your Personal iD was left blank. Did you not
   want any personalization?
4. Your Personal iD contains profanity or
   inappropriate slang, and besides, your mother
   would slap us.

If you wish to reorder your NIKE iD product with a
new personalization please visit us again at
www.nike.com

Thank you, NIKE iD

From: "Jonah H. Peretti"
To: "Personalize, NIKE iD" <nikeid_personalize@nike.com
Subject: RE: Your NIKE iD order o16468000

Greetings,

My order was canceled but my personal NIKE iD does
not violate any of the criteria outlined in your
message. The Personal iD on my custom ZOOM XC USA
running shoes was the word "sweatshop."

Sweatshop is not:
1) another party's trademark,
2) the name of an athlete,
3) blank, or
4) profanity.

I choose the iD because I wanted to remember the
toil and labor of the children that made my shoes.
Could you please ship them to me immediately.

Thanks and Happy New Year, Jonah Peretti

From: "Personalize, NIKE iD" <nikeid_personalize@nike.com
To: "'Jonah H. Peretti'"
Subject: RE: Your NIKE iD order o16468000

Dear NIKE iD Customer,

Your NIKE iD order was canceled because the iD
you have chosen contains, as stated in the previous
e-mail correspondence, "inappropriate slang". If

you wish to reorder your NIKE iD product with a
new personalization please visit us again at
nike.com

Thank you, NIKE iD

From: "Jonah H. Peretti"
To: "Personalize, NIKE iD" <nikeid_personalize@nike.com
Subject: RE: Your NIKE iD order o16468000

Dear NIKE iD,

Thank you for your quick response to my inquiry
about my custom ZOOM XC USA running shoes. Although
I commend you for your prompt customer service, I
disagree with the claim that my personal iD was
inappropriate slang. After consulting Webster's
Dictionary, I discovered that "sweatshop" is in
fact part of standard English, and not slang.

The word means: "a shop or factory in which workers
are employed for long hours at low wages and under
unhealthy conditions" and its origin dates from
1892. So my personal iD does meet the criteria
detailed in your first email.

Your website advertises that the NIKE iD program is
"about freedom to choose and freedom to express who
you are." I share Nike's love of freedom and
personal expression. The site also says that "If
you want it done right… build it yourself." I was
thrilled to be able to build my own shoes, and my
personal iD was offered as a small token of
appreciation for the sweatshop workers poised to

help me realize my vision. I hope that you will value my freedom of expression and reconsider your decision to reject my order.

Thank you, Jonah Peretti

From: "Personalize, NIKE iD" <nikeid_personalize@nike.com
To: "'Jonah H. Peretti'"
Subject: RE: Your NIKE iD order o16468000

Dear NIKE iD Customer,

Regarding the rules for personalization it also states on the NIKE iD website that "Nike reserves the right to cancel any personal iD up to 24 hours after it has been submitted." In addition, it further explains: "While we honor most personal iDs, we cannot honor every one.

Some may be (or contain) other's trademarks, or the names of certain professional sports teams, athletes or celebrities that Nike does not have the right to use. Others may contain material that we consider inappropriate or simply do not want to place on our products. Unfortunately, at times this obliges us to decline personal iDs that may otherwise seem unobjectionable. In any event, we will let you know if we decline your personal iD, and we will offer you the chance to submit another." With these rules in mind, we cannot accept your order as submitted. If you wish to reorder your NIKE iD product with a new

personalization please visit us again at
www.nike.com

Thank you, NIKE iD

From: "Jonah H. Peretti"
To: "Personalize, NIKE iD" <nikeid_personalize@nike.com
Subject: RE: Your NIKE iD order o16468000

Dear NIKE iD,

Thank you for the time and energy you have spent on
my request. I have decided to order the shoes with
a different iD, but I would like to make one small
request. Could you please send me a color snapshot
of the ten-year-old Vietnamese girl who makes my
shoes?

Thanks,
Jonah Peretti

<no response>

As one forwarder writes:

... this will now go round the world much farther and
faster than any of the adverts they paid Michael
Jordan more than the entire wage packet of all
their sweatshop workers in the world to do...

I normally avoid making a plea to pass on these
things, but this time I say: JUST DO IT

Beginnings

So how did viral marketing end up with its name? In my experience, a lot of people get concerned about it as they often confuse it with email viruses, so this is a good time to point out that they are two totally different things. Viral marketing, as already mentioned, involves someone choosing to send a message to a friend or colleague and therefore being in control. A virus, by way of contrast, is where you are sent something unwillingly and, as some virus programs do, you then end up sending the virus without your consent, on to other people whose addresses you have stored on your PC. OK, granted, that person who initiated the virus on purpose for some sad and very sick joke made a conscious decision to send it out, but hopefully you get the point! It gets its viral name in that it is contagious as it spreads, very quickly, from one to many.

And where did it all start?

There seems to be an industry-wide acceptance that the first real example of viral marketing was by Hotmail and in fairness, from a commercial point of view this appears to be true. However, before outlining Hotmail's success, there's a great UK example that beat even them by a couple of years, and even this particular case study was based on a similar campaign that took place way back in 1986.

In early 1994, Justin Kirby, now Managing Director of Digital Media Communications Limited, but then a mature student of the University of North London (UNL), together with his colleagues Paul Ryan and Ross Golden-Bannon launched a 'media virus' campaign. Kirby says they borrowed the term 'media virus' from the Douglas Rushkoff book of the same name (Rushkoff, D. (1994) Ballantine Books *Media Virus: Hidden Agendas in Popular Culture*). Their campaign was

designed to generate coverage in newspapers, radio and television of what they believed to be the severe and far-reaching effects of the cuts that the government of the time was making in student grants.

The aim of the campaign was to encourage students across the country to bombard the national media with telephone calls and faxes seeking coverage of the grant cuts.[9]

Kirby explained that their online tactic was used to create an offline activity.[10] The *Guardian Education* supplement described these tactics in detail by explaining that those who the students considered had failed to respond positively were targeted for further phone calls and faxes on their advertising lines hoping to jam them and cause serious disruption. At the same time they would barrage the switchboard at the Department for Education and the Treasury.[11]

The campaign was based on similar activities carried out by French students in 1986, who used the Minitel communications network, installed in large numbers of private homes, to muster support for their action. In Kirby's case, he used JANET, the Joint Academic Network, which was a computer grid that linked universities and colleges, and which student publications were able to plug into.[12] At the time, Kirby was editor of *Fuse*, the UNL student magazine, so was very aware of how to maximize JANET's capabilities. He therefore used email to coordinate a campaign between local action committees on campuses around the country, sending posters and handbills to his campaign colleagues, encouraging them to pass them on in the same manner.

Now helping to develop successful viral marketing campaigns for clients such MTV and Microsoft for the launch of their Xbox games console, Kirby believes his 1994 viral marketing campaign was a success but is disappointed that students in the UK do not continue to use the tactics he employed. He believes that his way is more effective than a march down Park Lane in central London. He achieved his aim of spreading a 'media virus' as his message was featured in the *Guardian* and the *Daily Telegraph*, as well as on national TV and local radio stations, all starting from a few emails on the then only electronic communication tool available to him.

It was two years after this before viral marketing reached the commercial sector with one of the industry's favourite success stories, Hotmail. Part of the success of this company is put down to the inspiration of one of its initial investors, Tim Draper, that drove Hotmail to 10 million users in less than 18 months.[13]

Draper's company, Draper Fisher Jurvetson, met with Hotmail founders, Sabeer Bhatia and Jack Smith in 1996 and invested $300,000 in the venture.[14] But according to Draper and Jurvetson, the special catalyst for Hotmail's torrid growth was viral marketing – due to the way it powerfully compounds the benefits of a first-mover advantage.[15]

One of the key reasons why Hotmail's success was achieved so easily was due to Tim Draper suggesting that they should include an advertising message at the end of every email: 'P.S. Get your free email at Hotmail'[16] – the last word of which also linked to the Hotmail website. As Draper and Jurvetson explained, this was very contentious at the time. Would users baulk at having this automatic addition to the content of their private messages? They eventually made the link less of a promotional plug by removing the 'P.S.'. However, all outgoing emails still had the one-liner advert at the end of them which continued to act as what Jurvetson and Draper describe as a 'subtle implied endorsement by the sender'. Their belief was that the recipient knew that the sender was a Hotmail user

and that this new free email thing seemed to work for them. Each new user became a company salesperson and the message spread organically.[17]

The power of viral marketing is quite possibly summed up in these two statistics from Draper and Jurvetson's Hotmail case history:

● Hotmail is the largest email provider in Sweden and India, despite the fact that it has done no marketing of any sort in these countries.

● Hotmail is used in over 220 countries, despite the limitation that it is only available in English.[18]

So there you have it, a new marketing buzzword was born and but a few years later, marketing managers from all aspects of business were worried that if they did not have a viral plan in place, they were missing something from their strategy. But viral marketing has come a long way from being a few emails sent across university networks or a tagline at the bottom of an email. Marketers are now exploring every which way to develop their emails to ensure that the content is worthy of its recipients passing it on. Do they simply produce a text-based message or develop it in HTML (the coding behind web pages). But what if the user's email is not HTML enabled? Should they just attach an image or document to the email? If so, how big should it be? Let's face it, if someone is downloading their emails from home on a slow modem, they won't be too happy waiting for a large file that they didn't request. Should it be an interactive game? Aren't email users now frightened of opening anything received as an attachment for fear of getting a virus? And what about all those compa-

Viral marketing has come a long way from being a few emails sent across university networks or a tagline at the bottom of an email.

nies that don't let their employers receive attachments to their emails for that exact reason. Finding the right formula for a successful viral email is not easy. And as the market has developed from those early days of the launch of Hotmail, companies know they need to be innovative to ensure that they cut through the mass of other emails that arrive in someone's inbox each day.

Before starting out, you need to understand whether a viral marketing campaign is appropriate for you anyway. For example, during one workshop I gave at a PR agency, an account manager said that she wanted to create a viral marketing campaign for her client. After asking just a few simple questions, it turned out that her client sold a product that had a market of approximately eight people in the UK. The account manager knew exactly who these people were and where she could find them as she had their company addresses and phone numbers as well as their email addresses. I therefore questioned who exactly she expected them to forward a viral campaign to who would be relevant for her client to speak to. A short time into the brainstorm, we agreed that, by all means, there might well be a case for developing a direct email campaign with a call to action in it. However, just because viral marketing happens to be the latest buzzword, it does not mean that it is appropriate to every marketing campaign. Viral marketing is about creating a reason for someone to pass a message on to someone else and, in this particular case, there was no one else of relevance to pass it to.

Therefore, once you've decided viral marketing *is* appropriate to your business, the challenge is to find the answer to that proverbial marketing question – how can we achieve just a small percentage of that early success of Hotmail?

KEY POINTS AND TOP TIPS

- Viral marketing is a new route to reach your target audience.
- Just as in any other marketing activity, you must understand who your audience is, where you can find them and what will entice them to take interest in your brand, product or service before embarking on a viral marketing campaign.
- For viral marketing to work, you must understand what will motivate your target audience to pass on a message to someone of similar mind and interests.
- Viral marketing is word-of-mouth marketing via a digital platform that can spread exponentially.
- Viral marketing can work both for and against a brand.
- Anyone, even with no available marketing budget, can generate a successful viral marketing campaign.
- Viral marketing is not appropriate if you have a finite number of people who your campaign will appeal to, especially if you have the ability to contact them all directly.

CHAPTER 2

Can I tell you a secret?

- Human communication
- Attitudinal influences
- Memetics and ideaviruses
- Emotional and motivational group behaviours
- Key points and top tips

Human communication

One of the factors that make humans stand apart from the rest of the animal kingdom is our ability to communicate about things that have absolutely no relevance to achieving those primary needs required to live. In fairness, it may be possible that whales and dolphins speak to one another about what a rough sea they've just swam through and how bad the rain is that afternoon – we really don't know. However, in the main, communication in the animal world is about survival. Yet, we, the human race, seem to want to communicate with our fellow men and women about anything and everything. And technology, in particular the internet and now wireless communication, has given us the opportunity to communicate with one another across the world, instantly and cheaply.

Communication in the animal world is about survival.

Email and SMS have exploded the level of communication that occurs between people. According to the Mobile Data Association, MDA, there were 992 million text messages sent across the UK's four GSM networks during July 2001, almost

doubling the number for the same period of the previous year, when 516 million 'chargeable person-to-person messages' were sent across the UK.[1] These figures reported by MDA brought the UK's annual text messaging total for the period ending July 2001 to 6.2 billion, roughly 32 million messages per day.[2]

Email and SMS New Media technologies have provided the opportunity in which viral marketing can thrive.

Traditional word-of-mouth marketing can take time for a message to spread. Think about it from your own point of view: how often do you pick up the phone to all your friends, let alone see them.

Granted, as a marketer I can get a message broadcast to a relatively large audience via radio or TV. But unless the listener or viewer has a tape or video recorder and owns their own broadcast media channel, they are limited to how much they can then do with the message by themselves, without the help of a large organization and some serious financial support. They could post the message through the mail, starting chain letters perhaps. Either way, it's going to take time. The same can also be said for the printed media. See something in a magazine or newspaper and perhaps you can photocopy it and stick it to every tree in your neighbourhood.

Email and SMS, however, have provided us with the ability to pass on a message instantly, to anyone else we know anywhere in the world.

In fact, I know from personal experience how easy it is to end up on the distribution list of a friend of a friend's email because you were both on the list when the mutual friend sent a message only a day earlier. Suddenly, this means you are not only passing on messages to people you know, but also to people you've never met before, but who are happy to receive a message from you because you know one of their friends. Seth Godin calls this second-, third- or fourth-order connections. He gives an example of receiving an email in his inbox from someone who is married to someone he went to summer camp with 20 years ago, who got his email address from a friend of a friend. Godin says that it's hard for him to imagine this person contacting him if he had to walk across the village and bang on his door or if he had to pick up a phone and call him. However, the moment any of us connects to the internet, we all connect to one another. And those connections make ideas travel. Fast.[3]

A great example of how these second and third connections work in terms of viral marketing is in a campaign that The Ministry of Sound ran in 2000. The club encouraged users to continue to pass on a particular email, ensuring they were kept informed, but also ensuring that the history of the referring messages was kept within the email. This was crucial to the campaign as the incentive to take part was that the email with the most people linked within it won a party at the nightclub for everyone who had been a part of that particular chain. Apparently, the winning chain had the names of over 1,000 people on it – who no doubt enjoyed a great night at the club!

Attitudinal influences

As well as enabling us to spread messages very quickly, perhaps more importantly, email enables us to influence a recipient's way of thinking about something in particular. This is why viral marketing has become an important part of a campaign strategy, when relevant of course, as it can have a huge influence on people's attitudes towards brands, products and services. As Allport pointed out (Allport, F. H. (1924) Houghton Mifflin, Boston *Social Psychology*), while our attitudes are a form of pre-programming, they are by no means innate or static. He said that attitudes continue to develop with learning over time and their four principle sources are our exposure to information, the environment we exist in, our group membership and, finally (and most importantly to viral marketing), our want for satisfaction. Allport outlined the difference between a group of people and a crowd by the fact that within a group, individuals are brought together for the purpose of deliberate activity, whereas a crowd is driven by motives of the more primitive and prepotent level. Allport stated that within a group, the individual's behaviour is influenced by perception of others engaged in the same activity.

When relating group behaviour back to the internet and wireless communications, it becomes evident how important it is to win over those individuals within the group who influence the views of others. These people who have the ability in some cases to make or break a product or service's success were identified by Public Relations agency, Burson-Marstella, as 'e-fluentials' in a 1999 US study that they carried out in collaboration with RoperASW.[4] According to the report, e-fluentials comprise 10% of the US online adult population and, compared with the average internet user, are far more active users of email, newsgroups and bulletin boards as well as other online communication tools. While influential online, they also give their opinions offline. However, it is the online medium that enables them to reach much further, both directly and indirectly, than they could in the real world because their opinions can, as we know all too well, be forwarded from one person to another quite easily. While this research was carried out in the USA, my belief is that this is just as relevant to the UK too, given that our online activity is not too dissimilar.

Burson-Marstella's 2001 report highlighted six key points about e-fluentials:[5]

1. They project their opinions far beyond the score of their individual contacts – imparting an experience to 14 individuals on average.

2. They spread news describing a negative experience to a wider audience than they do a positive experience. For example, they will pass positive experiences to 11 people on average compared to sharing negative experiences with 17 people on average or 55% more people than their endorsements.

3. Men seek opinions and provide advice on technology, while women e-fluentials primarily search for information pertaining to food and health and encourage others to take an active interest in women's issues.

4. They research before purchase, including both product information and other people's opinions.

5. They enjoy visiting company websites to gain information on brands, products and services.

6. They respond to direct email campaigns, whether solicited or not. However, the positive responses tend to be from known sources, i.e. brands that they trust.

It's all well and good understanding the importance of the e-fluentials, but how do we go about finding out from our databases who we should contact first to help spread the good name of the company and its products or services? According to Idil Cakim, Director in the Knowledge Development Group at Burson-Marstella, there are methods that can be employed to achieve this. In response to my question Idil explained that they can redirect visitors from Brand X's company website with a pop-up message to an e-fluential's quiz area on their own site. Here they have a complex and proprietary algorithm behind a mini-quiz, which allows them to differentiate between those who are e-fluentials and those who are not. The evaluation is based on the frequency of conducting a mix of the listed activities. After qualifying and identifying those visitors who are e-fluentials, they then work with this list of e-fluentials (of Brand X) by targeting them in communication campaigns that they design. For instance, they can advise Brand X on developing a close relation with these powerful opinion leaders and get their e-fluentials to be loyal, responsive customers (i.e. customers who purchase, customers who return to the website, customers who respond and forward unsolicited emails).[6]

It's not difficult to see how e-fluentials can have an impact on our own online activities. After all, if you receive an email from a friend or colleague with a link to a website and they've specifically told you to take a look at it, as you'll find it really interesting, why would you not believe them? And besides, if it's as easy as pointing your mouse and clicking on the link within the email anyway, to find out if they were right, then for the sake of those few seconds, you may as well try it. In 2000 56% of those surveyed for Forrester's UK Internet User Monitor had already been driven to websites by viral marketing.[7] Incredibly, however, a year after that particular survey, e-commerce sites were still failing to use viral marketing to attract customers and build their brands, according to Jupiter Media Metrix. Their research showed that only 7% of companies go to the trouble of tracking email pass-along rates, even though 45% of consumers choose online retailers on the basis of word-of-mouth

Would you be so quick to look at something if it came directly from a commercial company ...?

recommendations. They believe that customer acquisition costs can be reduced by 27% if viral marketing campaigns are used.[8]

The key factor in all this in terms of marketing is that it is the person who sent you the initial email who has endorsed the message. They've told you it's good and worthwhile looking at. Would you be so quick to look at something if it came directly from a commercial company that you hadn't requested information from or from someone who you didn't know? Doubtful!

Memetics and ideaviruses

So why do we pass on these messages so willingly and why are people so easily influenced?

The research for this book has led me to a relatively new science called memetics, which I found to be closely linked to viral marketing as it provides a good insight into the human psyche as to why we are influenced by others.

Memetics is the study of memes (pronounced *meems*) and was first introduced by Richard Dawkins (Dawkins, R. (1989) Oxford Paperbacks *The Selfish Gene*). Just as in biology, genes replicate themselves and are passed on through birth. Memes are replicating units that are passed from brain to brain, or mind to mind, that then cause the recipient to alter their own behaviour through replication or imitation, thereby passing on the meme to a further individual. According to Richard Brodie (Brodie, R. (1996) Integral Press *Viruses of the Mind*), people who understand memetics will have an increasing advantage in life, especially in preventing

If you better understand how your mind works, you can better navigate through a world of increasingly subtle manipulation.

25

themselves from being manipulated or taken advantage of. If you better understand how your mind works, you can better navigate through a world of increasingly subtle manipulation. And let's face it, as marketers embarking on a viral marketing campaign, that's the end result that we are trying to achieve.

Dawkins states that memes can be tunes or melodies, catchphrases, fashions, icons and slogans. A meme can also be an idea, as long as it has been passed on to someone, causing that person to repeat it to someone else. Therefore, it can be argued that all knowledge passed on from one person to another is memetic. Some memes will only exist for a short time such as fashions and fads, whereas others may last through generations, such as religions and nursery rhymes.

We do not need to search far to find some excellent examples of memes in the marketing world. Niké's tick logo is one of the most recognized in the world and, as an example of influencing others, it is so fashionable, some people have even had it tattooed on their body. And as for slogans, or catchphases, how many times do people, when ending a conversation with a friend, now say: 'You are the weakest link, goodbye'? Or when struggling to find the answer to a question say: 'Can I phone a friend?', each time reminding us of the latest quiz shows to take the world by storm.

Dawkins says that memes should be regarded as living structures, not just metaphorically but technically. He believes that when you plant a fertile meme in my mind, you literally parasitize my brain, turning it into a vehicle for the meme's propagation in just the way that a virus may parasitize the genetic mechanism of a host cell. He gives the example of where the belief in life after death has become so strong that it is actually realized physically, millions of times over, as a structure in the nervous systems of people all over the world.

Using ideas similar to the meme, Seth Godin describes ideas that move, grow and infect everyone they touch as 'idea-viruses'. He believes that if you can get people to accept, embrace, adore and cherish your ideas, you win! You win financially, you gain power and you change the world. According to Godin, in the new economy, consumers have built up antibodies that resist traditional marketing, which is why, as marketers, we need to stop marketing *at* people and start creating an environment in which consumers can market *to* one another. This is, therefore, evidence of the need for viral marketing in the marketplace.

Emotional and motivational group behaviours

So what are the human emotions and motivations that we need to exploit to enable us to influence our target audience's attitudes and behaviour and cause them to pass on our viral marketing messages?

As we've previously seen, we should be looking initially at the same principles that we consider in all other aspects of marketing and gaining a basic understanding of what motivates individuals to take the action that will achieve the goal of fulfilling their needs. In terms of viral marketing, these motivations are emotional, i.e. influenced by friends, families and colleagues.

With viral marketing, we should also put particular emphasis on how people behave within groups, as the key to a good viral campaign is the reliance on an individual forwarding a message to a large number of people at the same time. This is how campaigns spread exponentially and can travel round the world, 'virtually', three or four times in the space of 24 hours. One of the reasons viral campaigns work so well is that lots of

people have numerous friends' or colleagues' emails grouped together, so that forwarding a message to all those people in one go is very simple. These groups of emails will be similar to the groups that people join within the workplace or socially where individuals identify closely with others in the group. Behaviours are then affected as these individuals strive to be associated with the group and conform to the group norms. This then leads to peer pressure where our behaviours result from the need to be popular within the group, loved or understood. How many of us have sent at least one joke on to someone else the minute we've finished reading it? Come on. Own up! Care, however, must be taken in what is forwarded, as within these reference groups there may be certain kinds of behaviour that are approved of and some that are taboo. For example, as I was writing this book, I came across an example of how trying to pass on a viral marketing campaign can backfire on an individual if it breaks the taboo of the group.

As already mentioned, I started writing this book while in the USA. While I was there, one of the worst atrocities imaginable happened. Two planes were flown into the World Trade Center in New York, one into the Pentagon in Washington and one crashed outside Pennsylvania as the direct result of terrorism. Messages of condolences were immediately sent to an email group that I belong to – uk-netmarketing.[9] However, one individual thought it appropriate to send a message to the group wondering 'when the first "Nuke the Afghan" viral flash game would appear' and, unfortunately, one individual responded with a link to one such type of game. However, with members of the email group actually based in New York, and one responding to the posting commenting on the distaste of it, it was clear that the original posting was not well received. The viral element of it would cease within the group and the thoughts towards the company that started it and the individual who forwarded it to the group would become extremely negative. Care must be taken before starting any marketing campaign but especially one where you are relying on your audience to do your marketing for you. Understanding the group's dislikes is possibly more important than knowing what does interest them.

Not surprisingly, a short time after that message about Afghan-related viral campaigns was posted, there in my inbox lay the first Bin Laden-related email, shortly followed by SMS messages on my mobile phone. As I was writing this book, I continued to receive email after email with attached images, text-based jokes, links to Flash animated websites and downloadable games. What amazes me, especially when a disaster such as this has happened, or when someone famous dies, or is found guilty of a crime, is the speed at which these emails are put together and then worked around the world. In the short time after the Twin Towers collapse, I saw images that bordered on the sick to those that some might have you think are part of the propaganda machine from the USA. These included pictures of Bin Laden's face superimposed on the screen of the TV programme 'Who Wants to be a Millionaire?' asking the question of what chance he had of seeing it past Christmas.

Propaganda through viral email, now there is a thought. The cynics and conspiracy theorists among us will say that 'they' send out these images, whoever 'they' are of course. But someone is creating them. Who and **Propaganda through** why, if there is no fame or prize at the **viral email, now there** end of it, however, is beyond me. Per- **is a thought.** haps it's simply self-glory in knowing their work has found its way around the world. I suppose the main issue, however, is whether it matters how highly offensive these images are if they succeed in

their objective of getting the target audience within the country in a 'kick ass' mood. If they are highly effective in altering the attitude of their target audience to how the sender wants them to be thinking, surely they are deemed a success.

As I said previously, timing is all important when dealing with an issue such as the one just described, especially when using email. Once an email is let loose on the internet, if it gets into the wrong inboxes (those of people you would prefer were not targeted), the original author might just regret sending it, such is the power of the viral mechanism. This is something that Jo Moore, adviser to UK Transport Secretary Stephen Byers, discovered when she sent an email to Labour MPs after the World Trade Center had been attacked, but before the towers collapsed, urging colleagues to bury bad news in the fallout from the US terror attacks. Tony Blair denounced her comments as 'horrible, stupid and wrong' and during the days that followed, 25 Conservative MPs tabled a Commons' motion urging Byers to sack Moore forthwith for her 'sickening behaviour'.[10] While she made a public statement saying: 'I want to again sincerely apologise for the huge offence I have caused by sending this e-mail',[11] her future career and self-esteem were in the balance. She went on to say: 'I fully understand people's disgust at what I wrote. It is something I wish I'd never done and indeed find it difficult to believe I did. It's something I'll have to live with for the rest of my life. I can't take it back – no matter how much I wish – this terrible error of judgement.'[12]

So what *does* turn people on to encourage them to pass on a message in the first place?

There is a slide that seems to turn up in numerous presentations I have seen at various conferences – sometimes on more than one occasion on the same day. It refers to Ralph Wilson's

Six Principles of Viral Marketing, which state that an effective viral marketing strategy must contain one or more of the following:

1. gives away products or services
2. provides for effortless transfer to others
3. scales easily from small to very large
4. exploits common motivations and behaviours
5. utilizes existing communication networks
6. takes advantage of others' resources.

Wilson states that a viral marketing strategy need not contain *all* these elements, but the more elements it embraces, the more powerful the results are likely to be.[13] What would be interesting is whether or not he would stick to the statement that, as he explained while expanding on the first principle: 'Free attracts eyeballs. Eyeballs then see other desirable things that you are selling, and, presto! you earn money. Eyeballs bring valuable e-mail addresses, advertising revenue, and e-commerce sales opportunities.'[14] If only it were that simple! Two years on from when his article was published, we have seen numerous dot.com companies go out of business following a strategy of starting life by giving away free content in the hope that they would build revenue through selling additional services to registered users or simply through advertising. Unfortunately, this strategy has, in the main, failed. There was a time when first movers may have benefited from this strategy – Hotmail being a classic case in point. Draper and Jurvetson state that the typical viral entry strategy is to minimize the friction of market entry and proliferation with an eye to building in hooks and barriers to switching for customers. If the service is trying blatantly to monetize its subscriber base in every way imaginable, new users will be reluctant to spread the word.[15] In fact, they state that when they first invested in

Hotmail, they could not say with certainty how they would ultimately monetize their subscribers.[16]

There is no doubting that freebies attract users, but in the online arena it should not be treated as given that this will automatically lead to revenue and profit.

The one principle of Wilson's that, in my opinion, stands out above the others is that of exploiting common motivations and behaviours. As humans, our needs are made up of biogenic and psychogenic needs. A biogenic need arises from a biological condition such as hunger, thirst, cold or sickness and a psychogenic need arises from a psychological condition such as the desire to look attractive, the desire to be popular or the desire to appear prosperous.[17]

The main reason for our passing on a viral marketing message to someone else refers to the psychogenic need, stemming back to our need to communicate with other people. The majority of us long to be accepted as part of a group. Whether that group be the family, friends, colleagues at work or wherever, the motivation to gain acceptance is paramount in achieving our satisfaction. If we can pass on something to someone else that will be of benefit to their work, make them laugh or even give them the chance of winning something, then there is a greater possibility that we will become more popular with those people.

This chapter has highlighted the need to understand the motivators that are appropriate for the group that you are targeting for a viral campaign to become a success. I would always recommend, therefore, that before embarking on any viral campaign, due to the fact that, by its very nature, it could spread exponentially to either your benefit or detri-

As with any good campaign, the planning is just as important as the implementation.

ment, you research your audience first. As with any good campaign, the planning is just as important as the implementation.

Arguably, the best place to research your audience is either online or through their mobile phones, given that these are the channels that you will be using to communicate with them in any viral campaign. Understanding the way in which they respond, as well as the speed, can only help your cause and these methods are often regarded as a more cost-effective way for getting instant opinions from people. For example, to gain the research for the next chapter of this book, I used online market research site Tickbox.net which, at the time, had around 8,000 subscribers, representing a good sample of the UK population, who have registered with the site to take part in incentivized surveys. When they register with the site, users give personal information including age, gender and region, so that each time they return to complete a survey, they only need to log on and the site remembers all their details. This means that survey results can be pulled off at any time with full analysis automatically represented in clear graphs and tables. In offering an incentive of a prize of a balloon flight for two when the Tickbox.net newsletter was sent to its mailing list, I received around a 10% response in a very short space of time, enabling me to get an instant understanding of internet users' opinions of viral marketing.

There are numerous other online services as well as Tickbox.net. For example, NOP runs something very similar. However, if you do not want to use agencies such as these two, you can still create a simple survey on your own website to drive visitors to, so as to collect some basic information from them.

To get more detailed information, I would always recommend running focus groups with your target audience. Again, there are specialist agencies that handle these activities, as there is a certain skill in getting people to share their views in person or in groups and their not responding in the way they think you want them to. Focus groups will not give you the mass in terms of numbers of responses, but you will get more detailed information from a select few people.

I do not believe there is a golden rule as to which way round you run these types of activities. You can use focus groups to home in on specific findings from a survey. However, you can also use surveys to find a larger sample's views on an issue highlighted in the focus group. The important point is that you carry out at least some research of your target audience, rather than going on gut feel.

One thing to note is that to research under-16 year olds you require parental consent – another thing highlighted in the next chapter.

KEY POINTS AND TOP TIPS

- Encourage participants to include second, third, fourth and nth connections as incentives within a viral campaign, although be sure to consider opt-in clauses before contacting them again.
- Emails received from friends, family or work colleagues can have a major influence on the recipient's attitudes towards brands, products and services.
- Email enables us to influence more people than does word of mouth.
- Before embarking on a viral campaign, understand what motivates the individuals within the group that you are targeting by researching them.
- Lots of people have friends' or colleagues' emails grouped together making the forwarding of messages to lots of people instantly extremely easy.
- People want to be accepted within their groups and so will pass on messages for this reason.
- Some topics remain taboo within a group and if raised via email can have damaging implications to the recipients' perception of the sender.
- Timing is all important if a campaign is news related.
- Viral marketing is not just about giving away a free product or competition opportunity.
- Viral marketing is about exploiting common motivations and behaviours among groups of people.
- Email users will pass on a viral marketing campaign due to their psychogenic needs, relating to the desire to look attractive, be popular or appear prosperous and the need to communicate with other people and belong to a group.

CHAPTER 3

You've got mail

- Kids' and teenagers' use of technologies today
- Birth of email
- Consumers email behaviour
- Key points and top tips

Kids' and teenagers' use of technologies today

Email – can't live with it, can't live without it!

After subscribing to friendsreunited.co.uk, the site I mentioned in my introduction, I attended a reunion at my junior school. I left the school 23 years ago and revisiting it brought back some incredible memories. Were the chairs and desk really that small?

The one thing that struck me more than anything, however, was that, within all the same classrooms, rooms that had hardly changed since the school had been built some 100 years earlier, were now networked PCs all the way around the sides of the rooms.

I then thought about the fact that kids growing up and learning at school today know only of a world that includes the

Email – can't live with it, can't live without it!

internet and, of course, email. No longer do they need to wait weeks for a letter back from their penpal, so that, by the time you read their responses to your questions, you've forgotten what you asked in the first place. Kids today are instead growing up in a world where they can have conversations with 'emailpals' (if that's what you call them) instantly, all over the world. They can join chat rooms so that groups of friends can all chat together and, with some websites, they can even create their own virtual characters, called avatars, build their own virtual apartments and invite their friends round for parties – all online. All this has a major impact on how we market to them and emphasizes the importance of viral marketing particularly to this sector.

Latest research by Jupiter MMXI has found that Europe's 6.7 million online teenagers have a willingness to share information online. Their study found that 38% of respondents shared information they found on the internet, including photos, jokes, music files and greeting cards several times a week.[1] Teenagers are highly affected by the opinions and recommendations of their peers and marketers would do well to ride on the back of this, especially given that this is a time of their lives when their potential brand loyalty is being developed.[2]

Having said all that, according to Sarah Boorman, Marketing Coordinator in Cartoon Network's UK Interactive team, first-hand experience of having to market to teenagers by email has proved that it's not that simple. There is a lot to consider in terms of both how kids will react to being marketed to via email and the legal implications that go along with targeting under-16 year olds where data collection is concerned.

Cartoon Network follows strict legal guidelines ensuring that, when an under-16 year old wants to join their mailing list, parental consent is sought.[3] You would think that, from a viral marketing perspective, this would slow the process of increasing the mailing list down quite considerably. However, according to Boorman, parents normally give their consent within a week, although in most cases the turnaround time is actually a few days.

If data collection is a prerequisite of the email campaign, Cartoon Network will ask the child for not only their own email address but that of their parents too. The child is not allowed to provide the same email address; this is not acceptable. However, if there is only one email address available from the child, then Cartoon Network will send a letter in the post to their parents, if the home address is given, requesting written consent.[4] While the cynics among us might argue that by simply asking for email consent, there is a major loophole waiting to be exploited by devious teenagers, Boorman believes this is no different from a child faking Mum's or Dad's signature on a written letter. In fact, she says that the only certain way to be 100% confident is to capture data only at live events, where both child and parent are present.

By continuing with the online method of recruitment, rather than just live events, Cartoon Network has grown its database of under-16s significantly, 82% of which are from the UK, with a male-to-female ratio of 70:30. However, the importance for Cartoon Network's marketing team is that 54% of the mailing list are in fact, what Boorman calls 'mailable', i.e. the company has permission to contact them. Almost all the others on the list are awaiting parental consent other than a very small number – less than 1% - whose parents have refused permission for them to join the mailing list, for reasons, unfortunately, unknown.[5]

Having collected the data, Cartoon Network can sell access to companies wishing to run a third-party promotion, although they cannot sell the actual names and email addresses. They do have, however, strict internal guidelines as to which commercial partners are allowed access to the data and will vet

any emails that are asked to be sent, along with any website or campaign that the emails refer to.[6]

Interestingly, the number of 14 and 15 year olds who apply for parental consent to join the Cartoon Network UK mailing list is considerably less than that of their younger peers. In fact, the core age of the list is 10 years old. Boorman believes that this could be due to the fact that having to ask your parents for permission as you approach 15 years old is certainly not deemed 'cool' and perhaps it's better not even to bother to join! This results in Cartoon Network being unable to market directly to a proportion of the target audience for their web-site. However, the viral marketing aspect of any of their email campaigns counters this. If data collection is not an objective, then there is nothing stopping kids from passing on the emails to their friends, thereby helping to build the Cartoon Network brand among their peers and reinforce the message that Cartoon Network is there and it's funny.[7]

At the moment, Boorman believes that getting kids to visit a website through an email is quite difficult and that kids are more likely to discuss favourite websites in the playground than on email. She therefore feels strongly about the brand building aspect of email and would prefer to deliver a Flash or HTML email with a 'Forward to a friend' script within the email itself, than try to drive kids to a website to achieve the same aim. This recently worked very well for her, with a campaign the Cartoon Network Interactive team ran for the Cartoon Network Animation Awards in September 2001. The email that was sent to their mailing list had the subject heading, 'NEED CASH? GOT FLASH? THEN WIN THIS AWARD!!!'. On opening the email, the recipient was welcomed by a Flash movie and a very simple message:

"Cartoon Network Online Animation Awards – the only award for online animators that GUARANTEES TV exposure, £10,000 prize money and internet distribution for the winners.**"**

But key to the email's success was that there were only two actions the recipient had to make:

● To find out how to enter your animation: CLICK HERE

● To pass this onto your animator mates: CLICK HERE[8]

How simple!

Obviously, bypassing a website in a viral marketing campaign becomes a bit of an issue if click-through is an objective. However, for Boorman, where targeting teenagers is concerned, viral marketing is best used to reinforce the message rather than drive traffic. If it's purely branding that is needed, then kids can forward an email to their friends without any data collection required and hence parental consent no longer becomes an issue.[9]

But it is not just email, PC-networked classrooms and computers in the home that have changed the way kids communicate. No longer is there a need pass notes on bits of folded paper around the back of the class while at school. Why go to such lengths when almost all children have their own mobile phone which they can text one another on, using SMS, throughout the lesson.

In April 2001, according to NOP, 56% of the UK's kids aged 7 to 16 years owned a mobile phone, with this number rising to 77% when surveying only 14 to 16 year olds.[10] And while school teachers may not be happy about kids having access to mobile phones during lessons and are banning their use during the lessons themselves, they will have difficulty in banning kids from bringing them into school altogether. Parents

will feel more secure in the knowledge that their children have their own mobile phone from which they can make a call should they ever be in any danger or distress. They will, therefore, be happier that the kids have their mobiles with them on their journeys to and from school.

Birth of email

These findings highlighted for me the fact that the way in which we all communicate has changed dramatically over the last few decades and, while SMS is growing, email has certainly had the biggest influence. In the UK, 12 million people have access to email, sending or receiving about 180 million messages a day, with research company Vanson Bourne estimating that by 2005, 400 million emails will be sent every day in the UK alone.[11] But just what must US engineer Ray Tomlinson have been thinking when, in the autumn of 1971, he wrote the 200-line program that started it all off?[12] Could he seriously have imagined what was about to explode out of this invention?

In the UK, 12 million people have access to email, sending or receiving about 180 million messages a day.

Silicon.com celebrated email's 30th birthday with an article that discussed how Tomlinson's program allowed a user to send a message to any computer hooked up to Arpanet, the forefather of the internet, which was developed by the US Department of Defense. It told how a program he had written allowed files to be sent to and from the interconnected machines and then how he developed this by writing a messaging program to distinguish between messages addressed to the mailbox of a local machine and those connected via Arpanet. The symbol he chose to act as a differentiator between messages was the @ character. According to

Silicon.com, the first message was likely to have been sent between two machines resting side by side and containing the message QWERTYUIOP (the top line of letters on the keyboard) in capital letters, although Tomlinson himself says he can't remember exactly what the message was.

Tomlinson didn't actually invent email itself. That had been around since 1965 when Fernando Corbato and colleagues at the Massachusetts Institute of Technology developed a program to let the individual users of the institution's Compatible Timesharing System (CTSS) swap messages. But that program only let people using one machine communicate with each other. Ray Tomlinson made it possible to swap messages between machines in different locations; between universities, across continents, and oceans.[13]

Today, it seems we can't live without email. From a business point of view, it's instant, cheap, flexible, enables you to speak to numerous people at the same time, you can use it to gain information, survey and sell, as well as many other important functions of a company. From a consumer's point of view, you can keep in touch with friends, family, apply for jobs and organize parties. The opportunities are endless. And that is exactly where the problem arises for the marketing professional.

With email so easily accessible, so cheap and being used so frequently, how do we get our marketing messages heard above the noise of all the other hundreds of messages that arrive in our audiences' in-trays each week?

According to *Director Magazine*, the most active 40% of business users send an average 40 emails a day – yet on average, much more is received.[14]

The emails we receive will tend either to be personal, i.e. from friends, family, loved ones or colleagues at the office arranging

the lunchtime drink or they will be work related. Mixed in with these will be those that form part of a 'spam' campaign. These will be where somehow, someone has either got hold of your email address or guessed it correctly. They have then sent you an unsolicited email, normally asking you to sign up to a way that can make you a million dollars very quickly or recommending that you visit a website where you can see some adult entertainment! From my own experience, these are the kinds of email that tend to clutter up your Hotmail account. There will also be those that you have requested to receive, i.e. mailing lists or direct email campaigns from companies you have opted into to receive more information from (or not opted out of, whichever the case may be). At some stage it may be that you receive a virus email, which may be from friend or colleague, but as described earlier in the book, was sent unintentionally. And finally, of course, somewhere in your ever-increasing inbox, there needs to be room for those viral email campaigns sent out by us marketers.

Jupiter speculates that 268 billion advertising email messages will be sent in 2005 – an increase of 2,200% from 2001.[15] As consumers, if we continue to be bombarded by so many such messages, we will simply continue to press delete each time we receive them. This highlights the importance of viral marketing. If we can achieve the goal of encouraging someone to endorse our message by forwarding it to a friend or colleague, there will be more chance it will be opened and read, given the name in the 'From' field is recognizable.

Consumers' email behaviour

So what do the public think about it all? In January 2001 a survey carried out by Lowe Live and BMRB suggested a significant fall in the numbers of people who continue to forward viral emails. In a sample of over 1,000 internet users, of the 64% who received marketing emails from companies, only 13% forwarded them. However, the belief was that viral marketing would see a resurgence once the majority of consumers were online.[16] Ten months after this (a lifetime in internet years) I decided to find out if attitudes had changed. As part of my research for this book, I carried out a survey of UK internet users using independent online research site, Tickbox.net. The survey was responded to by just under 800 people, who were asked to provide answers to the following questions:

1. Could you live without email?

2. Could you live without SMS/text messaging on your mobile phone?

3. How do you contact your friends the most?

4. Do you ever open files that are attached to your email?

5. Have you ever visited a website by clicking on a link within an email sent to you by a friend or work colleague?

6 Do you ever forward emails that you've received to friends or work colleagues?

7. Do you ever forward SMS/text messages that you've received to friends or work colleagues?

8. What would make you view an attachment to an email or click on a link within an email sent to you by a friend or work colleague?

9. What would make you forward an email to a friend or work colleague?

Finally, I asked participants in the survey to tell me about the best email or SMS/text message they had received that they had then passed on to a friend or colleague.

My findings make up the remainder of this chapter.

Could you live without email?

Of respondents to this question, 69.4% said they could not live without email, which I must admit, I found to be lower than I had anticipated (see Figure 3.1).

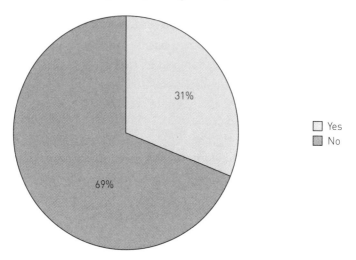

Figure 3.1 Number of respondents who could not live without email
Source: www.tickbox.net, November 2001

However, when broken down by gender, it is apparent that women are more dependent on email than men, although only just! Of the women, 72.5% couldn't live without email compared to 64.8% of men (see Figure 3.2).

As the age increases, people are, perhaps not surprisingly, less dependent on email. However, it *was* surprising to see that more people between the ages of 25 and 34 years are dependent on email than the 16 to 24 year olds.

I believe it is fair to assume that the former group of people is more likely to be at work. It is possible that they have grown up and started their working life with email being an everyday part of it, whereas the younger age group perhaps may not be so reliant on email if they are not working at all or not as

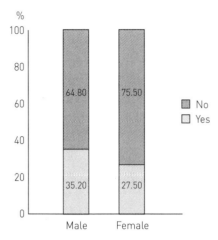

Figure 3.2 Age dependency on email
Source: www.tickbox.net, November 2001

much. What is evident, however, is that as people get older, they are less reliant on email, but I find it amazing that, of those who are over 55 years old, 57.6% said they could not live without email (see Figure 3.3).

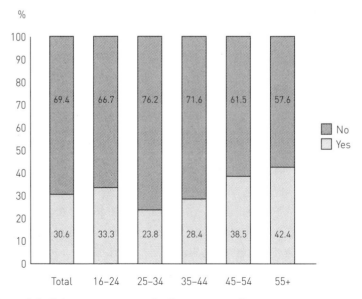

Figure 3.3 Older age groups and reliance on email
Source: www.tickbox.net, November 2001

Could you live without SMS/text messaging on your mobile phone?

Given that SMS is a relatively recent phenomenon, the following figures are really quite staggering. From the entire sample in the survey, 32.6% could not live without SMS on their mobile phone. However, 14.8% of the sample didn't actually have a mobile, so when you discount these people from the sample, of those with mobile phones, the number of people who could not live without SMS actually rises slightly, to 38.3% (see Figure 3.4).

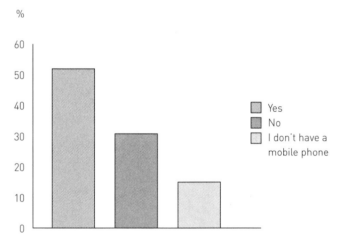

Figure 3.4 SMS and text messaging on mobile phones
Source: www.tickbox.net, November 2001

On this occasion, the difference in the genders is quite significant. Of women from the entire sample, 35.6% said they couldn't live without SMS on their mobile phone compared to only 25.9% of men. Again, when we consider the results of only those who own a mobile phone, the figure for women who can't live without SMS rises to 40.9%, compared to 31.7% of men.

However, it's when we start to break the results down by age range that they become really significant.

Of 16 to 24 year olds across the entire sample, 61.9% could not live without their SMS messaging, with only 9.5% of this age group not owning a mobile phone. Therefore, when looking at the number of mobile phone owners in this age group who couldn't live without SMS, the figure rises to an astounding 68.4%.

In terms of mobile phone ownership, aside from a slight dip in the 25 to 34 year old age bracket, where 9.1% of these people do not own a mobile phone, the percentage continues to rise through the ages as 16.1% of 35 to 44 year olds, 16.9% of 45 to 54 year olds and, finally, 34.8% of 55+ year olds do not own a mobile phone. In reverse to this trend, as the age of any one group rises, these people become less and less dependent on SMS messaging. When concentrating just on those people who do own a mobile phone, the percentage of them who rely on SMS messaging decreases from 48.9% of 25 to 34 year olds, to 31.3% 35 to 44 year olds, 20.3% of 45 to 54 year olds and, finally, just 9.3% of those over 55 years old (see Figure 3.5).

How do you contact your friends the most?

Is technology a good thing or a bad thing when it comes to speaking to our friends? It's great to be able to stay in touch, but wouldn't it be nice to see each other once in a while? Only 15.8% of people surveyed stay in contact with their friends more so by actually seeing them. Not surprisingly, speaking on the phone is the most popular way of staying in contact, but only just. The survey revealed that 39.4% of respondents use the phone most to stay in touch, but email is

49

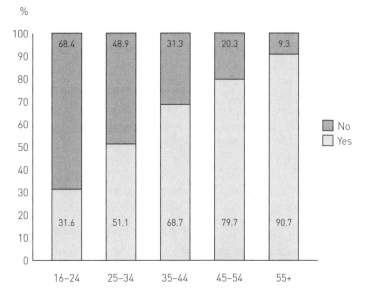

Figure 3.5 Age and ability to live without messaging
Source: www.tickbox.net, November 2001

only just short of this figure at 30.4%; while 14.3% use SMS more when staying in contact with friends (see Figure 3.6).

However, when we investigate how they compare across gender, there is a noticeable difference in the use of SMS messaging across the entire sample, compared with seeing friends. Women are more likely to contact their friends through an SMS message than they are actually to go to see them – 16.7% against 11.9% respectively, as compared to the men, where only 9.6% of men would contact their friends using SMS more than any other method. Women also contact their friends more compared to 23.3% who would actually see their friends more. Women also use email and the phone more than men to contact their friends the most: 31.5% of women use email most to contact their friends, as compared to 29.6% of men and 40% of women use the phone most to contact their friends as compared to 37.4% of men (see Figure 3.7).

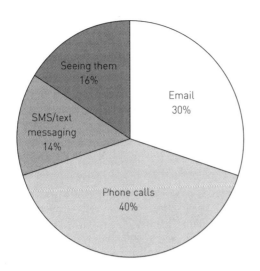

Figure 3.6 Breakdown of how we contact friends the most
Source: www.tickbox.net, November 2001

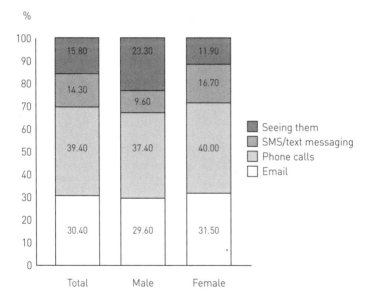

Figure 3.7 Women's and men's differing methods of contacting friends
Source: www.tickbox.net, November 2001

Where we do see significant differences is in the regions. In the Carlton TV region – that is, London – email becomes the most used method to contact friends, with 41.4% of this group using this method, as compared to 37.1% using the phone, and 15% use SMS, meaning, quite sadly, that in the London region, only 6.4% get out enough to contact their friends more through seeing them!

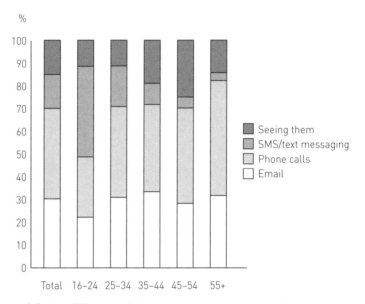

Figure 3.8 Age differences in how people contact one another
Source: www.tickbox.net, November 2001

However, once again, the most variances occur when we investigate the differences in the age groups. Whereas in the entire sample, SMS is the least popular method of contacting friends the most, as far as 16 to 24 year olds are concerned, it becomes the most important, with 39.3% of the sample in this age group contacting friends most by SMS. This then drops considerably through the ages, with 17.5% of 25 to 34 year olds, 9.3% of 35 to 44 year olds, 6.8% of 45 to 55 year olds and a measly 3% of 55+ year olds using SMS as the method of contacting friends the most. As age increases, the phone becomes more popular rising from just 25% of the 25 to 34 year olds, to twice as many 55+ year olds, at 51.5%. Email, however, stays quite consistent. Aside from a dip in 16 to 24 year olds, with only 23.8% saying they contact friends most using email, the rest of the age groups do not differ significantly from the population average of 30.4% (See Figure 3.8.).

Do you ever open files that are attached to your email?

The first three questions established the fact that a significant amount of the UK internet population can no longer live without email or SMS, together with the fact that they use it a considerable amount of time to contact friends. Now we will look at the really interesting information that will have a major impact on how we actually develop the strategy behind our viral campaigns in the immediate future.

The results of this question were extremely encouraging given the spates of viruses that have hit the internet.

At more and more meetings that I have with clients and PR agencies, the questions arise that, when planning a viral marketing campaign, is it wise to attach something to an email, or are you better off sending HTML or text-based emails? Well, the good news, according to my survey, is that only 2.4% of respondents said they do not receive attachments to their emails and 7.7% said they never open attachments to their email. Furthermore, 46.4% said they sometimes open attachments and 33.1% said they do so most of the time, leaving 10.4% of respondents saying that they always open an attachment when they receive it on their email (see Figure 3.9).

There is very little difference between the attitudes of men and women when looking at whether or not they open attachments to their emails: 11.1% of men always open their attach-

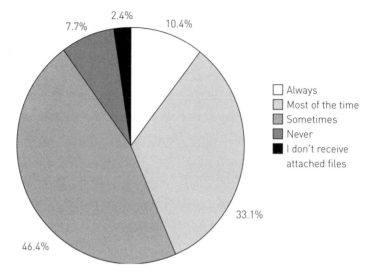

Figure 3.9 Who opens attachments to their emails?
Source: www.tickbox.net, November 2001

ments compared to 10.2% of women, whereas 7.8% of men never open an attachment compared to 7.3% of women.

From a regional point of view, Londoners again seem to like using their email, with 18.6% of the Carlton region always opening their email attachments, whereas in the Granada region in the north west of the country, only 6% do. In the central region, the number of people that always open email attachments drops even more significantly to just 3.6%. However, the encouraging piece of information is that the huge majority of people will at least sometimes, if not most of the time, open an attachment.

Once again, where we see the significant differences in attitudes is across the age brackets. More than twice as many 16 to 24 year olds, 22.6%, compared to the overall population will always open an attachment, whereas the older population must be more security conscious, with 15.2% of them saying

they never would – almost twice as many when comparing across the entire population of the survey. Sixteen to 24 year olds were also significantly more likely to open an email attachment most of the time compared to the rest of the population (see Figure 3.10).

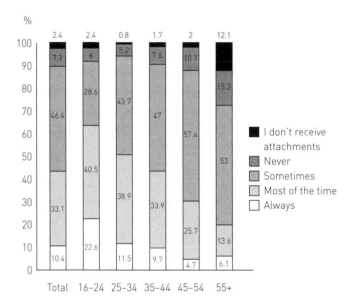

Figure 3.10 Age and likelihood of opening attachments to emails
Source: www.tickbox.net, November 2001

Have you ever visited a website by clicking on a link within an email sent to you by a friend or work colleague?

If the findings from the answers to the previous question were encouraging for anyone arguing the case for viral marketing, then the findings provided here will confirm its need in the marketing mix. A staggering 84.2% of those surveyed said they had visited a website by clicking on a link within an email sent to them by a friend or work colleague. Only 13% said they hadn't, with the remaining 2.9% unsure either way! (See Figure 3.11.)

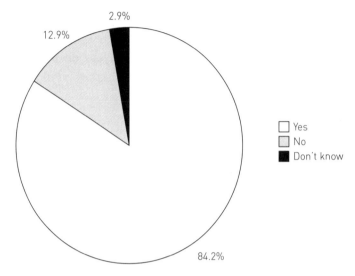

Figure 3.11 Visiting a website through a link in an email
Source: www.tickbox.net, November 2001

The results were even more positive where targeting men is concerned, as 87.8% of men had visited a website by clicking on a link from a friend's email, whereas only 82.3% of women had.

What was also interesting is that, when studying the Carlton region, once again our friends in the south show how email friendly they are, with 89.3% of the survey population based in the Carlton region having clicked on links in their friends' emails, whereas in the Granada region, only 77.4% had – although this is still a significant amount, of course.

Once again, however, the clearest indication of how more likely someone would be to act on a viral marketing campaign is reflected in the age group. In the 16 to 24 year old age range, the figure is again 89.3% who said they had clicked on a link within a friend or work colleague's email, with this figure rising to over 90% when studying the 25 to 34 year olds. It then drops significantly as we go through the older age groups, with 81.8% of 35 to 44 year olds, 79.7% of 45 to 54 years olds and, finally, only 71.2% of 55+ year olds having clicked on an email link. What could be seen as something to be more concerned with when studying this older group is that over 10% of them didn't know either way! (See Figure 3.12.)

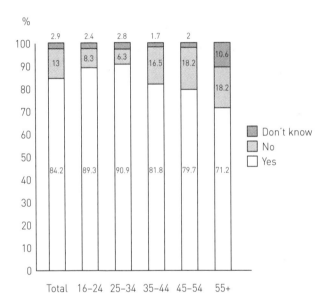

Figure 3.12 Age and usage of links in email attachments
Source: www.tickbox.net, November 2001

Do you ever forward emails that you've received to friends or work colleagues?

While still encouraging, there is certainly some work still to be done to convince a number of internet users to forward emails. I would not expect many people always to forward a message, as I would not anticipate its always being relevant to anyone else. However, seeing the number of people who never forward a message received from a friend or work colleague to

someone else grow to as much as a third in certain sectors means that we have to look closely at how we develop viral marketing campaigns targeted at these groups. Obviously, there is still some way to go to convince this large number of people to do what we want them to do and spread the word of our products or services! (See Figure 3.13.)

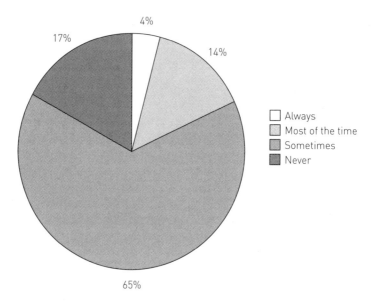

Figure 3.13 Forwarding received emails to friends and colleagues
Source: www.tickbox.net, November 2001

Out of the entire sample, 3.5% of people said they always forward these types of email, 14.2% said that they do so most of the time, 65.5% some of the time and 16.7% said they never do.

There is very little difference in the behaviour of men and women when it comes to the responses to this question. However, women are slightly more likely to forward a message received from a friend or work colleague as only 15.8% of

women said they never had done so before compared to 17.4% of men.

Once again, the most significant findings are in the differences between the ages, with the older generation again showing they are not as susceptible to viral marketing as the younger market. Not one respondent aged over 55 years old said they always forward a message received from a friend or work colleague and a significantly high proportion of this group, 33.3%, said they never do. Whereas in the 16 to 24 and 25 to 34 age groups, both scored lower percentages than the survey population in terms of never forwarding a message, with the figures of 6% and 10.7% respectively. There is some concern, however, when we target anyone over 45 years old with a viral marketing campaign. At this age level, the number of people who never forward a message reaches a quarter, with exactly 25% of 45 to 54 year olds saying they never had either! (See Figure 3.14.)

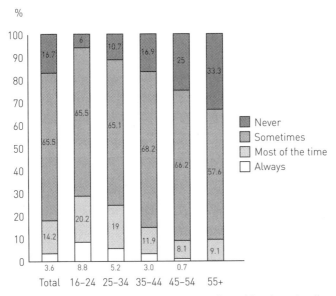

Figure 3.14 Age and forwarding received emails to friends and colleagues

Source: www.tickbox.net, November 2001

Do you ever forward SMS/text messages that you've received to friends or work colleagues?

From the findings of this survey, it looks like viral marketing has still got some way to go before it takes off on the mobile phone. Of all respondents, 49.4% had never forwarded an SMS they had received. Yet when we discount the 16.9% who said they didn't have a mobile phone when answering this question, of the remaining people who do have mobile phones, the amount of people who never forward an SMS they have received to friends or work colleagues rises to 59.46%. Only 1.9% of the entire sample said they always forward SMS messages to friends or work colleagues, 4.8% said they do most of the time and 27% said they sometimes do (see Figure 3.15).

What was interesting from a gender perspective was that considerably more women, 52.7%, had never forwarded an SMS

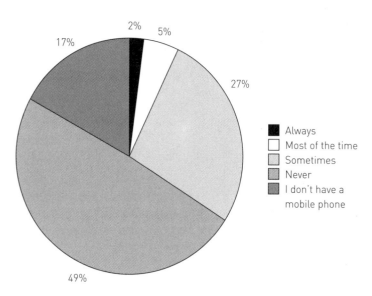

Figure 3.15 Forwarding SMS/text messages to friends and colleagues
Source: www.tickbox.net, November 2001

message to a friend or work colleague compared to the men, of whom 44.4% never had (see Figure 3.16).

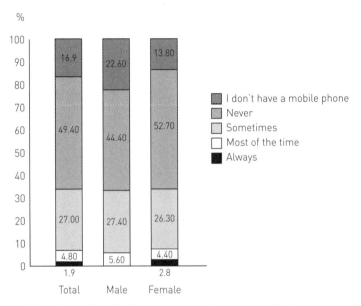

Figure 3.16 Forwarding SMS messages and the gender divide
Source: www.tickbox.net, November 2001

Needless to say, and this was becoming quite consistent in the findings, the major differences in people's behaviours was discovered when comparing age groups. If we look only at the activities of the mobile phone owners in each age group, we find that, while out of the total survey population 59.46% have never forwarded an SMS to a friend or work colleague, 16 to 24 year olds are more likely to do so. The probability of this happening then decreases as the group ages, bar a small blip at the higher age bracket. This deviance could be put down to the fact that as such a large number of them didn't have a mobile phone, the sample size left to analyze was considerably smaller than the other age groups. Out of the mobile phone users on the survey, 39.47% of 16 to 24 year olds had never

forwarded an SMS to friends or work colleagues, whereas 50.22% of 25 to 34 year olds, 61.54% of 35 to 44 year olds and 81.8% of 45 to 54 year olds hadn't. From the 55+ age group, the figure was still significantly high, but had fallen back slightly to 75.61% (see Figure 3.17).

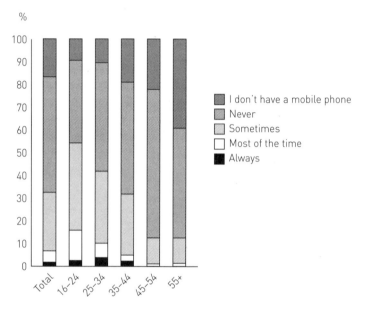

Figure 3.17 Age groupings and forwarding SMS messages
Source: www.tickbox.net, November 2001

What would make you view an attachment to an email or click on a link within an email sent to you by a friend or work colleague?

Now we are really getting into the minds of our audience in understanding what it is that will get them to open attachments or follow links sent to them by friends or work colleagues. Not surprisingly, the top three reasons were product recommendations (67.3%), giving them the chance to win a competition (65.9%) and due to its comical nature (58.4%). What did surprise me was how low a percentage of respondents said that sexual content was a reason for opening attachments or clicking on a link. Just 12.8% of respondents admitted to this! While Tickbox.net provides a certain amount of anonymity, I strongly believe that this is still not a true reflection of people's views and that a lot of people find it embarrassing to admit to viewing sexual content online – however harmless it might be. On reflection, I also feel that the wording of this statement may have confused some people. What some people may think of as just a little rude, others may deem sexual and it is also possible that some respondents may have thought I was referring to porno-graphic material.

The significant reason why people don't bother following links or opening attachments was superstitious chain mails – something that I recall seeing lots of in my early email days yet now, according to this survey, this interests less than 1% of people!

So basically, if you are going to create a viral marketing cam-paign that is untargeted, the order of importance for your incentives should be:

- It's a product recommendation.
- It gives you the chance to win a competition.
- It's of a comical nature.
- It provides you with advice/help.
- It helps your friend or colleague win a competition.
- It earns you money.
- It raises money for a charity.
- It joins a petition.
- It's of a sexual nature.
- It's a superstitious chain mail.

Unfortunately, you cannot please all the people all of the time and, in fact, there are some people you just cannot please at all! Of all respondents, 15.5% were not turned on by any of these reasons (see Figure 3.18).

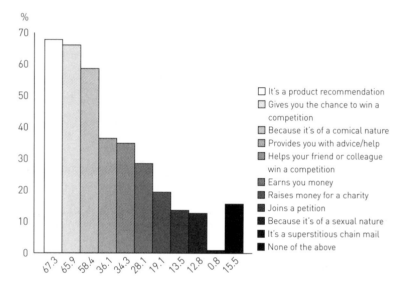

Figure 3.18 Why people view attachments or click on links within emails
Source: www.tickbox.net, November 2001

It's only when we look at the differences in responses to this question between men and women that we really start to understand – or reconfirm – their behavioural patterns. For example, men are more than twice as likely to view an attachment or follow a link from a friend's email if it's of a sexual nature – 19.6% of men and 9.4% of women said they would do. I doubt that this statistic is a surprise to anyone. And just as expected, women are more likely to join a petition or raise money for charity through email than men. Some 16.1% of women said they'd follow a link or view an attachment if it

were to join a petition, compared to 10% of men. Also, 23.4% of women said they'd do the same if it were to raise money for charity, compared to less than half the number for men – just 11.9%. Obviously, the latter are too busy looking at their sexually related emails! (See Figure 3.19.)

Once again, there are some significant differences in how the age groups respond to emails sent to them by friends or work colleagues. For example, a sense of humour is obviously

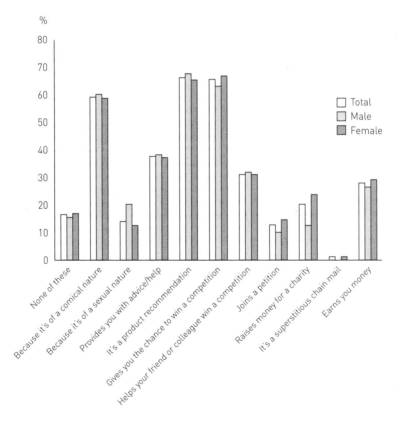

Figure 3.19 Clicking on links and forwarding messages and the gender divide

Source: www.tickbox.net, November 2001

something that we lose as we get older! Where 77.1% of 16 to 24 year olds would view an attachment or click on a link if it were of a comical nature, only 70.6% of 25 to 34 year olds would. However, as we go through the older ages, it gets even less: 52.5% of 35 to 44 year olds, 45.9% of 45 to 54 year olds and just 36.4% of those over 55 years old.

A similar trend occurs when looking at the statistics of who would react to something of a sexual nature. Over 22% of 25 to 34 year olds would act on something of a sexual nature. This, however, drops significantly to just 9.3% of 35 to 44 year olds, 6.1% of 45 to 54 year olds and just one person on my survey from the 55+ age groups – at least he (or she) was honest!

What is significant was the high percentage of people in the 14 to 44 year bracket who act on product recommendations, with 79.5% of 16 to 24 year olds and 73.5% of 25 to 34 year olds saying they would click on a link or open an attachment if it were a product recommendation.

Most of the other reasons were quite consistent across the age ranges other than joining a petition and raising money for charities, where the younger generation, those perhaps still willing to voice an opinion, were more active. If it involved joining a petition, 21.7% would act on an email as compared to the survey average of 13.5% and 32.5% would do so if it meant raising money for charity, compared to the average of 19.1%.

What would make you forward an email to a friend or work colleague?

Finally, the all-important question in terms of viral marketing. How can we get someone to pass an email on to someone else? Well, by far and away the leading reason why someone would pass on an email to a friend or colleague is to make them laugh – 78% of respondents said they would do this, compared to the next highest response of 49.6% who would do it to recommend something. Competitions then come into play, with 46.9% forwarding messages to include their friends and colleagues in winning a competition and 41.4% ensuring that they get to win one by doing so. After these top four reasons, there is a significant drop to 15.5% of people who would forward emails to earn themselves money and 14.6% who would do so to raise money for charity. Then, just over 10% of people would forward an email because of it was of a sexual nature, would make them feel appreciated or to encourage someone else to join a petition. Just under 10% would do it to embarrass their friends – obviously the person who sent me the .exe file that, on opening it, flashed the words 'I AM GAY' across my screen in big letters and bright colours must be in that 9.7% of people! Chain letters get the raw deal again with just four people from the entire survey saying this would be a reason to forward an email to a friend or colleague – thank heavens for that! (See Figure 3.20.)

Once again, we see the differences in moral standing between men and women when we compare some of these results. For example, more than twice as many men, 15.7%, would pass on an email because of its sexual nature compared to just 7.4% of women. Yet, when it comes to doing something of just repute, only 6.7% of men would try to get their friends or colleagues to join a petition, compared to 13% of women and 8.6% of men would do so to raise money for charity, compared to 18.5% of women (see Figure 3.21).

Not surprising then, that in the week while typing these survey results, I received such an email from a female work colleague. This particular message informed me that Thames Water had set up a website associated with 'Water Aid' and

would donate £100,000 (which will provide safe drinking water for life to 6,000 people in Africa and Asia) if they have 2,000,000 visitors to the site in 'the next 12 weeks'. Of course, it didn't say when the 12 weeks had started, so who was to know how long this message had been doing the rounds. However, the email pointed out that it only took a few seconds to visit the site and so asked me to click on the 'Click here' link and then pass it on to as many as people as I knew. Needless to say, being a man and now having access to my survey findings – you can work out for yourselves what I did with the email...

Continuing with my findings, we discovered that men would much rather embarrass their mates – 13.8% of them would anyway, compared to just 8.1% of women. Finally, the only other significant difference across the genders was that women are obviously more into trying to win competitions

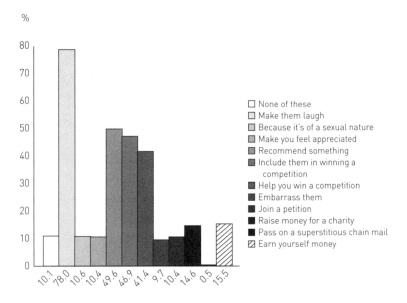

Figure 3.20 Reasons to forward on email to a friend or colleague
Source: www.tickbox.net, November 2001

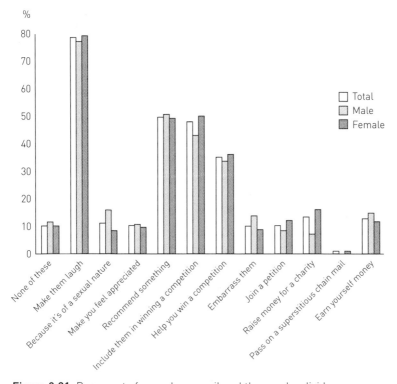

Figure 3.21 Reasons to forward an email and the gender divide
Source: www.tickbox.net, November 2001

online. Of the women, 50.9% would include their friends and colleagues in the winning spirit compared to just 40.3% of men and 42.3% of women pass on emails to help themselves win a competition compared to 39.2% of men.

Finally, the last quantitative piece of analysis from this survey reaffirms the findings of the previous question outlined, that our sense of humour diminishes as we get older. While 88% of 16 to 24 year olds will forward an email to friends or work colleagues to make them laugh and 87.2% of 25 to 34 year olds would do the same, the figure drops to 74.2% of 35 to 44 year olds. Then, quite alarmingly, as we get over the 45 year old mark, it drops again, to 69.4% of 45 to 54 year olds and,

finally, just 59.1% of those over 55 year olds would forward the email to make someone laugh.

Similarly, 16.8% of 25 to 34 year olds would pass on emails of a sexual nature, compared to less than half that number of 35 to 44 year olds at 8.3%. Just 6.3% of 45 to 54 year olds and, once again, just one of my over-55 year old respondents would do the same – I wonder if it was the same person as before?

Surprisingly, this trend is similar in forwarding emails that may make the sender feel appreciated, although not so when it comes to embarrassing people, where virtually the same trend occurs once more.

Where the over-55s do come into their own is in raising money for charity, where 19.7% of them would pass on an email to achieve this aim, second only to 16 to 24 year olds, at 24.1%. Both these groups are also much more likely than average to be interested in earning themselves money through forwarding emails to friends or colleagues (see Table 3.1).

What was the best email or SMS message you have received that you then forwarded to a friend or work colleague?

This final question left the respondents an open text field to tell me anything they wanted – and they certainly did. What was interesting for me was the fact that I had seen so many of them myself – perhaps as you read the list of some of the responses to this question, you might have some fun count-ing how many of these you've seen too – just to prove a point.

Emails

There was an interesting selection to say the least and obvi-ously, due to the timing of my survey, a number were related

Table 3.1 Age and reasons to forward an email

	Total	16 to 24	25 to 34	35 to 44	45 to 54	55 +
None of these	10.1%	1.2%	7.6%	13.1%	11.8%	18.2%
Make them laugh	78.0%	88.0%	87.2%	74.2%	69.4%	59.1%
Because it's of a sexual nature	10.6%	12.0%	16.8%	8.3%	6.3%	1.5%
Make you feel appreciated	10.4%	18.1%	12.8%	9.2%	4.9%	4.5%
Recommend something	49.6%	57.8%	56.0%	49.8%	36.8%	47.0%
Include them in winning a competition	46.9%	51.8%	48.8%	45.0%	43.8%	47.0%
Help you win a competition	41.4%	42.2%	46.8%	38.4%	36.1%	40.9%
Embarrass them	9.7%	19.3%	12.4%	5.2%	5.6%	9.1%
Join a petition	10.4%	10.8%	14.0%	7.9%	6.9%	10.6%
Raise money for a charity	14.6%	24.1%	18.8%	9.6%	7.6%	19.7%
Pass on a superstitious chain mail	0.5%	1.2%	1.2%	0.0%	0.0%	0.0%
Earn yourself money	15.5%	22.9%	15.2%	14.4%	11.1%	21.2%

Source: www.tickbox.net, November 2001

to the various Osama Bin Laden jokes that seemed to be working their way around the internet on an hourly basis. However, what surprised me, given the findings of the previous questions, is that there were hardly any responses that related to product recommendations. Also, while participants in the

survey didn't seem to be too forthcoming in admitting to reading and passing on emails of a sexual nature, most of their favourite ones they listed in this question related to exactly that! Unfortunately, most were simply too unrepeatable for this book.

My cousin sent me a funny email to remind me of my loved one. It was of an office worker in USA getting crabby with his computer and bashing it and then chucking it across the room. Don't we all feel like that sometimes!

An email, which included a jpeg of a woman with a big arse – the title was 'Does my skirt look big in this?'

Man eaten by snake

Smiling is infectious, you catch it like the flu. When someone smiled at me today, I started smiling too. I passed around the corner, and someone saw my grin, and when he smiled, I realized, I'd passed it on to him. I thought about that smile

New Geordie 'version' of Windows (Windaz). All the Window's options were in Geordie-speak... very funny!

An email containing a link to a website that claimed to have everyone's baby photograph – when viewed it was a photo of a monkey

It was a picture of a woman's remote control and a man's remote control

A video of a man getting his head stuck up an elephant's bum

A petition to help the women of Afghanistan who are living under a repressive regime

An email message from America with regard to the terrorism tragedy on 11th September – asking the people of UK (and other countries) to unite together to oppose the Taliban

Surfers, swimmers, snails, dreamers... Guinness promotion!

TV advert for John West

Tommy Cooper jokes... Just Like That!

It was a recommendation to try Tombola which I did and then won £84

It was a comical Christmas elf bowling game

A comical MSPowerpoint attachment about how to identify a mad cow

From an old school chum who got in touch via FriendsReunited attaching an old school photo, which I then forwarded to family and friends so they could have a good laugh at my very bad hair cut and toothy grin!

The hand

Please click this link and donate for free and save the rainforest

First time I ever saw an old lady kicking a pretend baby like a football

Email – advising a friend of a special flight offer

An amusing animated Christmas e-card

The best email which I have sent on was recent. It was an email which generates food for the people who have been affected by the terrorist attack in the US. I think that everyone should help with this

Congratulations you have won a trip to the Caribbean

Spoof press release stating that use of a vibrator was shown to decrease eyesight – message was sent in flickering text

The email telling me about this competition

Northern Budweiser sound bite

It involved a video clip of an aroused donkey and a guy trying to take a toilet break in its field

A list of the speed camera locations

Splat the MP

Virgin.com – free cinema tickets

It was from my brother-in-law and it was about a gerbil in a microwave

Fantastic email slagging off someone else in the office – but it was sent to me as well as the person in question. Since most of the office agreed with the sentiments contained in the email, it got circulated far and wide!

Virgin – Necker Island

SMS

Hi, it's me... I was wondering if I could stay with you for a while...everyone is so pissed off at me... I really need a friend. Sender: Osama Bin Laden

A picture of a bear and the text said gosh your mobile is advanced it now has a mirror installed

About American pie

Yahoo horoscope

It was a messaged that flashed that said if the message was flashing, you are in desperate need of sex!

A mate sent a message offering a full set of encyclopaedias for a fiver. He said he had no further use for them as he had just got married and his wife knew everything

National friends week chain letter

Flashing SMS teddy bear saying 'I love you'

I once had a ONE-TO-ONE with a virgin, she teased me till I got an ERICSSON, sucked me till my face went ORANGE, till I busted my load of SIEMEN over her NOKIAS. Sorry if it's a bit rude

Comical take on the weakest link and an Ascii picture to go with it

You are in my heart forever, with a flashing heart

KEY POINTS AND TOP TIPS

- Kids and teenagers today only know of a world with the internet and mobile phones.
- European teenagers are willing to share information online.
- Teenagers are highly affected by the opinions and recommendations of their peers.
- Parental consent is required to market directly by email to an under-16 year old.
- If you are not collecting data from under-16s there is nothing stopping them passing on your marketing messages to their friends by email or SMS.
- Viral marketing can be used to reinforce a brand message just as well as to drive traffic to a website.
- A large percentage of kids now have mobile phones.

- UK internet users can no longer live without their email and women are more reliant on it than men. The most reliant group is 25 to 34 year olds.

- Over a third of all UK mobile phone users could not live without SMS messaging and women are more reliant on the technology than men. However, two-thirds of 16 to 24 year old mobile phone users could not live without SMS, whereas less than 10% of over 55 year olds feel the same way.

- Almost half the internet population use either email or SMS to contact their friends the most with the percentage significantly higher when investigating just 16 to 24 year olds.

- Of UK internet users, 90% have opened an attachment to their email and less than 3% do not receive attachments.

- The huge majority of UK internet users have visited a website by clicking on a link within an email sent to them by a friend or work colleague.

- The vast majority of UK internet users will at some stage forward an email to a friend or work colleague although a third of 55 year olds never pass on an email.

- Viral marketing across SMS is significantly behind that of email as over half the UK mobile phone owners have never forwarded an SMS message.

- The top three reasons why someone would view an attachment or click on a link in an email they've received is because it's a product recommendation, a chance to win a competition or something funny. Superstitious chain mails interest hardly anyone.

- By far and away the biggest reason for people passing on an email to a friend or colleague is to make them laugh. Following this, the next reasons are to recommend a product or service and then to either include friends or work colleagues in winning a competition or to ensure that they win one themselves by doing so.

CHAPTER 4

Sex, lies and videotape

- Case studies introduction
- Sex sells
- Money for nothing and holidays for free
- Branding using viral marketing
- Video killed the HTML star
- SMS – technology of a new generation!
- You can't please all the people all of the time
- Key points and top tips

Case studies introduction

So who has succeeded in creating a decent viral campaign and what are the criteria for that success? In this chapter, I will take a look at some case studies, commercial and non-commercial, and try to analyze what was good, bad or downright ugly about them. These have not been picked for any reason other than they have either landed in my email inbox at some stage over the last couple of years, or I came across them during research for this book.

Sex sells

There's no doubt about it, whether the respondents to my survey in the previous chapter admitted it or not when discussing their email habits, I strongly believe that sex is a key motivator influencing some people's attitudes and getting

them to act on certain things! And in terms of online activity, I'm sure it doesn't take me to inform you that sex is something that also motivates a large proportion of the online community to interact. This, without doubt, includes passing on emails to friends with links to websites or attachments that include images and video files. However, obviously, I am in no position to comment how many of these are legal.

Sex is a key motivator influencing some people's attitudes and getting them to act on certain things!

What is important in terms of viral marketing is how to use sex or at least innuendo to your advantage from a commercial perspective, without crossing the line that has you shut down!

One company that has shown the way to achieve this, albeit with a business that revolves around sex, is the Australian online retailer, AdultShop.com. According to Amanda Cooper, their Head of Marketing, the reason that they can achieve this is that:

"The comical, cheeky and humorous nature of our brand opens up numerous opportunities, which translate effectively into viral marketing campaigns. The success of viral marketing initiatives hinges on the propensity of people to pass the content on, and for them to do this, it must evoke a strong response be it humorous, emotional, fear or the like. Our brand message is about making sex fun for everyone. Viral marketing lends itself perfectly to our approach."

Cooper added that: 'Viral marketing works well for AdultShop.com as the majority of people are more comfortable forwarding something humorous which is adult in nature online rather than admitting they were on our website or talking about it.'[1]

The following case study outlines one such campaign that was so successful that it worked its way around the globe.

AdultShop.com created an advert shot specifically for internet viewing, with the primary objective of promoting the company and gaining brand awareness through a viral marketing campaign. The ad, for a made-up product called 'Big Boy Briefs', features a man who, on any normal day, would fail to impress the girls. However, thanks to the fact that he is wearing his Big Boy Briefs, he has suddenly become rather more attractive. This is because, as the advert quite clearly demonstrates, the amazing AdultShop.com product manages to fool

Big Boy Briefs.
The pump-up
underpants.

the two female onlookers that a certain part of his anatomy has dramatically increased in size in front of their very eyes.

Cooper believed the Big Boy Briefs viral campaign was, to her knowledge, Australia's first tele-viral advertisement (TVA), a term coined by the company which, as she explained, means a television-type advertisement produced solely for viewing on the internet.[2] As it turns out, the incredible success of the campaign has meant that the advert did not end up as the exclusively online project it originally set out to be. In fact, it ended up being viewed on television as well, but to the joy, no doubt, of the company's financial director and bank manager, without the huge expense of having to pay for the airtime. PR success has resulted in some highly valuable offline 'exposure', to coin a phrase! Television coverage included 56 seconds of airtime on Australia's Channel 10 show 'Rove Live', with a media value of $56,000 (Australian). In Germany, the TVA gained 312 seconds of airtime on the VOX Channel show 'Wahre Liebe'. And finally, in the UK, London Weekend Television's 'Tarrant on TV', which at the time of AdultShop.com reporting on their success was receiving over 10 million viewers (47% of the UK audience at that time on a Sunday evening at 10pm), had promised to show the TVA in early 2002.[3] Also in the UK, the story has been featured in men's lifestyle magazine *FHM*.

The campaign aims were to take advantage of the 'forward to a friend' nature of email with specific commercial goals defined from the onset. These were to communicate the AdultShop.com brand; drive traffic to the three adultshop.com shops; increase opt-in members and drive sales; and finally to serve as new product development research. AdultShop.com chose viral marketing for a number of reasons. First, they believed that, by using this technique, their campaign had the potential to reach a global market extremely quickly. They also felt that there was a strong brand alignment with the technique in that 'sex and fun are at the core of most successful viral marketing campaigns and are also at the core of the AdultShop.com brand'. The belief was that the medium being used was free and measurable. And finally, their campaign involved low production costs, shooting on digital format and not film.[4] In fact, the entire campaign cost less than $10,000 (Australian) to produce.[5]

So how did they do it?

- Film clip shot and reduced to 1.5MB mpeg and Quicktime formats to circumnavigate compatibility issues.
- Landing page built including links to download clips, an email entry box for more information and tagged links to the three AdultShop.com stores.
- Text email sent to AdultShop's mailing list of approximately 30,000 names worldwide, including a link to the landing page.
- Rich media banners inserted into AdultShop's online banner advertising schedule to help 'ignite' the campaign.
- Entire clip mailed to friends and colleagues who expressed an interest.
- End frame of clip includes tagged URL adultshop.com/bigboy which directs users to the landing page where they are able to read more information about the product and have the opportunity to leave their email address and opt into the AdultShop.com newsletter.
- Traffic and sales monitored through the server log analysis and referrer ID tags included on shop links.[6]

Sarah Sproule, Adult Shop's Global Public Relations Manager, who developed the PR strategy surrounding the campaign, told me:

"Not only has the Big Boy Briefs campaign been extremely suc-cessful from a viral marketing perspective online, but it has also been instrumental in increasing the global brand aware-ness of AdultShop.com. This has been due to the media cover-age it has received around the world."

As well as finding its way on to global television, the viral marketing campaign also achieved its original aims of being, first and foremost, an online success. There were 61,000 unique visitors to the landing page during April 2001 and an estimated 50,000–75,000 views of the commercial globally a day. However, perhaps most importantly, the TVA also resulted in a positive return on investment with regard to sales driven from the landing page after just 25 days. Traffic and sales continued to increase after that time and the cam-paign acted as a catalyst for media awareness of the Adult-Shop.com brand on a global level.[7]

So why did AdultShop.com think that their campaign, devel-oped with Australian advertising agency, 303, worked so well. According to Cooper:

"The content of the campaign is comical which makes it well suited for viral distribution. This enables communication of the AdultShop.com brand on a global level, as viral marketing is not restricted by the geographical boundaries inherent in using traditional media. The brand building benefits a successful viral marketing campaign can generate for a company are sig-nificant. Also, the free media and quality of production for a rel-atively low cost allowed by this medium make it an extremely viable means of achieving this objective. With Big Boy Briefs we have 'piggy-backed' on the branding benefits of viral market-ing, using the campaign to directly drive traffic to the three AdultShop.com websites catering to the Australasian, North

American and German markets. This has the effect of increasing opt-in members and driving sales." [8]

OK, so perhaps not all of us have the advantage that, by creating a TVA with a sexual theme, we will directly drive our
audience to buy our products. However, the message here is
clear. Sex and comedy certainly sell. Have a campaign that
combines the two and you end up with a
pretty potent formula for getting people
to pass on emails and click on the links
within them. Content of a humorous, sexual or even innuendo nature will not be appropriate for every campaign and I
am certainly not suggesting that marketing managers should
be looking to include it within their next viral campaign. However, where they can get away with it, they certainly should.
For me, though, the clever part of the strategy is not just the
sex and the comedy. That is a given, as we've described earlier,
about motivational factors. What impressed me about this
campaign is the fact that this advert was shot exclusively for
the internet, thereby bringing the cost down and the content
creativity 'up'!

**Sex and comedy
certainly sell.**

Money for nothing and holidays for free

In this case study, we will discover how giving away something for free works to motivate people into passing on an
email. However, when considering such a strategy, care must
be taken in ensuring that you are not just acquiring 'hangers
on', i.e. those who are there just for the freebie and have no
intention of ever becoming a customer for good. This can be
partly avoided by the initial target list that your viral is sent to,
because, if we work on the principle that people will forward
it to those friends or colleagues of a similar mindset, your
wastage can be minimized. However, the very nature of viral

marketing means that you have less control over the more traditional techniques of marketing and PR. Therefore, as soon as word is out that there is something available for nothing, the viral campaign will spread extremely quickly to the masses.

Giving away something for free works to motivate people into passing on an email.

Both Thomas Cook and Virgin Wines discovered just how quickly a campaign could spread when, in the spring of 2000, they launched campaigns with similar strategies. On both these occasions, the key mechanic was driven via their websites, giving them the control over the viral send. Users had to enter names and email addresses of numerous friends so that they could also be included in the offer. This resulted in more than just the usual benefits of a viral marketing campaign for both companies. By directing users to a web page to forward on the message rather than relying on them to forward the message simply through their email, Thomas Cook and Virgin Wines gained the ability to add value to the campaign through data collection.

Thomas Cook's campaign was pretty straightforward in what it was asking users to do. Visitors to their website were invited to register their details in return for special offers, such as a weekend break where the guest pays only for breakfast and dinner, with the accommodation provided free. The viral element came from the fact that, in addition to registering their own details, visitors were also given the option of emailing the offer on to up to nine of their friends. By changing the offer, the company used the campaign to target different types of user, with different demographic profiles[9] and the result was that Thomas Cook generated 250,000 new customers through its Weekend Breaks email marketing campaign.[10]

The only concern would be how many of those customers actually remained loyal to the brand. For example, according to one source, the drop-off rate following subsequent emails to the new database was dramatic, although the end result was that even allowing for the fallout, the size of the database was significantly larger post-campaign than it had been pre-campaign.

The viral marketing campaign run by Virgin Wines had a slightly more inviting prize, but again, used the principle of directing participants to a website to take part and getting friends involved by entering their email addresses in the entry form. However, unlike the Thomas Cook campaign, where everyone was a winner, on this occasion, there was just the one big prize – albeit a pretty enticing one. The winners of this competition would get to spend a week on Necker Island, Richard Branson's private Caribbean hideaway.[11]

However, there was a very clever catch involved, which was potentially the key motivator to get participants to ensure those who they had passed the message on to visited the site and registered too. The idea was simple: if the friends you nominated to take with you on the holiday, should you have

won, didn't go back to the site and enter the competition themselves, your entry became null and void.

The two campaigns were certainly original at the time and, since then, many have appeared from other companies using similar mechanics. There is no doubting that both these campaigns were a success. However, I recall at the time many people commenting that 'enough was enough' and that there were only so many times an email from Thomas Cook or Virgin Wines could arrive in your inbox before it started to have a negative effect on your perception of the brand. The campaigns were potentially in danger of being victims of their own success as consumers, including me, started to get tired of the same email arriving day after day, either via the website or forwarded directly from someone else's email. Perhaps someone should research how many times a consumer can receive the same offer via email before they do begin to think negatively of the company making the offer to them.

If you were to follow this principle of getting consumers to email a web page, offer or competition on to friends or colleagues, then the situation of duplicated receipts can simply be avoided. There are companies that specialize in email marketing that have developed applications for their clients to run their own viral marketing campaigns through automated 'wizard'-based online systems. According to David Godden, Head of Professional Services at e2 Communications Europe Limited, one such specialist agency, their software runs off a database which initially 'dedupes' (checks for duplicate email addresses) the mailing list, ensuring that users do not receive the same initial email more than once. Then, as the campaigns are controlled via their own email server, when someone's email address is entered into the forward-to-a-friend box, the database simply looks to see if they have already been forwarded the campaign by someone else before sending it on.

Godden said that it would be simple to add a mechanism then to notify the referrer that the person they referred had already been sent the campaign by someone else and to ask whether they would like to send it to anyone else.[12]

Branding using viral marketing

Not every viral marketing campaign has to link back to a website to be classed as successful. Just as online banner advertising shouldn't just be measured on the number of people who 'click through', neither should viral marketing be measured on the traffic generated to your website.

The so-called 'demise' of banner advertising is a personal bugbear of mine. There have been so many reports on the fact that banner advertising is dead because average click-through rates have reduced to considerably less than 1%. However, there are a number of reasons why this may have happened and if the people who plan and buy the campaigns, along with the media owners who sell them, gave time to the placement, creative and timing, then click-through rates could be improved dramatically. However, the main reason I get so frustrated with comments around the death of the banner is that this viewpoint is often based purely on measuring a campaign's success by the click-through it generates to the brand's website. However, what if the objective of the campaign were to raise awareness of a particular product, event or promotion? For example, consider a scenario whereby a brand such as McDonald's has an objective to let its target audience know that its new 'Happy Meal' promotion enabled customers to receive a gift related to the latest Disney film. In this instance, would McDonald's drive the audience away from the website they have made a conscious decision to visit in order to deliver that message to them? Let's face it, it's pretty much

a given that we know McDonald's sells burgers and that it also sells Happy Meals. So unless I have a need to create a database of like-minded individuals that I can market to at a later date with special offers perhaps, I can simply achieve my objective by serving a creative banner advert, with no concern on the click-through generated.

In exactly the same light, the return on investment (ROI) of a viral marketing campaign and, therefore, its success should be measured purely against clearly defined objectives that are set out at the start. If one of those objectives happens to be increasing brand awareness (or brand association with an occasion or event), then viral marketing can achieve this without driving traffic to a website.

As an example, take a look at a game created by Denver, Colorado-based multimedia and game development company, Clever Media.[13] This is available on their website, but I received it virally a couple of years ago. Just as the company name suggests, they have created a clever application that provides a couple of minutes of fun. The idea is very simple and offers users a virtual challenge replicating the problems that all men face when desperate to use the toilet, but who find, to their dismay, that the 'gents' is not empty. Which urinal do you use? The game goes through six scenarios where you have to choose which urinal you would use on each occasion.

This is a superb use of the technology and a great use of viral marketing. The concept is simple – and it's funny. It is easy to use and only takes a couple of minutes to play. However, for me, while I'm sure this game has been very effective in driving traffic from the New Media and marketing industry to Clever Media's website, I can't help thinking that it would have been better used as a branding exercise for either a jeans or condom brand. Just imagine how many 'eyeballs' either

brand would generate with this working its way around the internet at speed. If I were asked to adapt this for such a company, I would use a subtle form of branding. Either company could very easily achieve this. If I were marketing a brand of jeans, for example, I could place my brand's logo on the back of some of the men's pockets as they stand by the urinal. Alternatively, if my aim were to promote the condom brand, I would perhaps place a dispensing machine on the wall in the background on each frame of the application. If, as an additional objective, either company still wanted to generate traffic to their websites, any placement of their logos could easily be made into active hyperlinks to achieve this.

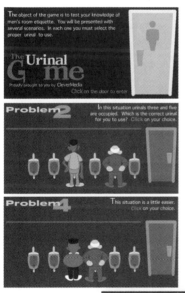

Video killed the HTML star

In true viral form, only recently, someone posted a message to the uk-netmarketing mailing list I mentioned in Chapter 2, about a website that allows you to view web pages just how we all did in the 'early days', using various browser emulators. The site is www.dejavu.org and I selected the good old NCSA Mosaic browser to view my company website. Mosaic was the browser I had on my Apple Macintosh back in 1994 when I was one of the very first few hundred thousand members of the UK online population. It's incredible how things have progressed in that short space of time. Plug-ins galore have come our way, all allowing the internet to become an interactive playground of sound, video and animation – if only those technical wizards could sort out delivering smell over the wires!

We've already discussed how video can have an impact in a viral campaign with the AdultShop.com case study we looked at earlier. However, in terms of measuring the effectiveness in detail of video or animation-based emails is concerned, US company MindArrow[14] seems to have found one possible answer. Their technology allows you to embed compressed video into emails without the need for plug-ins and they have shown in various case studies how this has the potential both to increase click-through and the referral rate. What's really clever, however, is the fact that within MindArrow's Messenger Suite of applications, you can create, manage, deliver and track the campaigns,[15] with reporting that allows you to monitor the click-through activity of those people who have had the initial email sent to them by friends. In fact, on a number of occassions, the click-though rate has improved when analyzing the activities of those who received the email as a referral. This is more than likely because of all the reasons we have discussed earlier in the book, about endorsement from friends and colleagues. However, MindArrow has continued to prove that interactivity within email can certainly help from a commercial perspective. According to their own figures, they register a 27% pass-along or 'viral' effect, which refers to the percentage of viewers who receive the MindArrow Message from a friend or colleague.[16]

There were two specific examples of this technology that impressed me the most that I felt really showed that if you get the right spokesperson on board providing you with a video message, there's a great chance of people passing it on to like-minded individuals.

The first example was to help promote the US release of Britney Spears' single 'Oops! I Did It Again'. Within the video that plays in the MindArrow 'e-brochure', Britney gets users to interact by saying: 'If you follow the links below you can win a trip for four to one of my concerts.' However, the main reason for the potential success of the viral aspect of this campaign is that she also encourages her fans to send the email to their friends by saying: 'You can also help spread the word by passing this e-commercial on to a friend.' Now, tell me, what Britney fan wouldn't pass on the message if she personally asked them to do so? This certainly is one of the best uses of a celebrity spokesperson in an online campaign that I have seen in all my years of online marketing – even if it is all done to promote her own record, of course! Oh, and by the way, she finishes off the message by saying: 'I want to thank all my fans from the bottom of my heart – you're the best in the world!' Ahh. Said with such sincerity! But if you were young and impressionable, you'd believe it all right.

The second MindArrow e-brochure is a great example of how viral marketing can work in a business-to-business environment. In this instance, Oracle Corporation promoted their

February 2000 E-Business Seminar by sending out a video clip of their Chairman, CEO and basically all-round godlike creature (if you are a devout Oracle user, that is), Larry Ellison, taken from a previous keynote speech that he had made. The key to this excerpt is that, if you understand the relationship that Larry Ellison has with his number one rival, Microsoft's Bill Gates, what he says becomes very comical. Within the clip, Ellison states: 'All information should go into a common database – why? I'll quote the most brilliant man I know – Bill Gates.' At which point the audience burst into laughter. Ellison continues: 'Who said "It's getting harder and harder to find stuff on my PC, maybe everything should be in a database so I can search for it".'

If you are an Oracle user, as we saw in the Britney Spears example, seeing the company's Chairman and CEO in action is a huge incentive to view the video and then, perhaps, budget allowing, register for the seminar. After all, as the clip of Ellison finishes, the video ended with the message: 'Don't be left out, register now', after which the e-brochure automatically opened a web browser, which, if you were online, took you to the web page which allowed you to register for the seminar.

As it's funny, you'd certainly want to pass it to colleagues and other people you know who also use Oracle. And finally, as part of the continual 'one-upmanship' that Oracle and Microsoft users go through, you may even want to send it to people who you know use Microsoft's products. All in all, this, again, is a superb execution of what could easily have stopped at just another direct email campaign, but by including the humour, video and, of course, 'Forward to a friend' script, it becomes viral.

MindArrow is not the only company in the USA to provide this kind of technology. Among other competitors, TMX Interactive also claims similar successful case studies. One such campaign was for Coreride, a retailer of high-end equipment for the snowboard, skateboard and extreme sports enthusiast, which boasted an incredibly high viral marketing effect, with over 40% of rich media emails delivered being forwarded to other email addresses. The reason for its success, the company believes, was because they created a highly visual, 30-second Flash email, that included a vibrant audio track to grab the attention of the sports extremists that they believed the campaign would appeal to.[17]

SMS – technology of a new generation!

As we have shown in previous chapters, SMS has arrived and it can be used to great effect for viral marketing. This was proved during the summer of 2001 when SMS marketing company, Flytxt, created a campaign for UK film distributor, Momentum Pictures to help promote the release of teen comedy, *Get Over It*.

The objective of the campaign was to create a buzz around the movie by building a dialogue with the female audience using viral and interactive text messaging over a six-week pre-release period prior to its launch. The primary objective of creating this buzz was to encourage more of the film's target audience to visit the cinema to watch the film, with a special focus on driving in an audience on the first weekend of release.[18]

Flytxt initially set about building an interactive text club of the core target market – female teenagers – by recruiting participants and then managing an interactive dialogue to promote the movie. This was achieved through interactive offline advertising (i.e. print advertisements that promoted an SMS number for subscription) in teen magazines *Bliss* and *J-17*. A poster advertising campaign was also run in cinemas and shopping centres, which also included cinema countertops. Finally, there was point of sale advertising in the cinemas, which also had full subscription instructions.[19]

The viral element to the campaign came in the shape of a game that encouraged members to refer their friends to the *Get Over It* text club.[20]

Once acquired, subscribers were invited to participate in a range of competitions related to the theme of the movie. These included sending in their best 'dumping' lines over SMS, which

gave them the opportunity to win items from the movie such as a bikini, similar to that worn by its female lead star. Subscribers would also receive latest news and gossip on the movie.[21]

Momentum Pictures chose the SMS viral route for a number of reasons. First, the teen movie leveraged a buzz around the anti-social trend among teenagers of dumping their girl-friends or boyfriends by SMS. The excitement would lead to interest about the movie as well as information about the release. It would therefore drive more teenagers to watch the movie. At the same time, they would build a database for future releases while establishing a channel for direct feed-back about the campaign and the movie itself.[22]

The results were superb and underline the importance that this new channel has where viral marketing is concerned, par-ticularly if targeting teenagers.

Momentum Pictures managed to build up what they considered to be a sizeable database and the company said that they 'were extremely pleased by the high response we had among our target audience of teenage girls'. The viral game, where the refer-ring of friends gave users the chance to win goodie bags, generated 17% addi-tional subscriptions. An impressive 69% of the club members participated in the dumping competition and finally, and possibly most importantly as far as the film company was concerned, the movie reached number three in the chart, behind *Pearl Harbor* and *The Mummy Returns*, which they felt was a fantastic achieve-ment for a teen movie.[23]

69% of the club members participated in the dumping competition and the movie reached number three in the chart.

At a recent Flytxt seminar, I was informed that if the initial SMS send is timed correctly, for example, hitting teenagers as

they leave school in the afternoon, you can watch the viral effect work immediately as subscriptions increase by 10% to 15% within the first few hours. This kind of information really hits home the message of how powerful SMS can be in the right environment and the role viral marketing has within it. This is truly a powerful medium, more powerful perhaps than email could ever be. Let's face it, when we leave home now, we check for our keys, our wallets and our mobile phones! And soon we will not even need our wallets. All transactions will be through m-commerce – so long as our mobile phone battery has not run out, of course!

Soon we will not even need our wallets. All transactions will be through m-commerce.

We have only seen the start of the SMS explosion. However, I believe the industry has a duty to control the level of marketing that is carried out using this method, especially where under-16 year olds is concerned. While entry to competitions via SMS or subscriptions to services referred to by your friends may only cost a few pence each time, it is already clear there are concerns at how kids are becoming addicted to this technology. If kids are given the opportunity to enter tens or even hundreds of competitions easily and subscribe to any number of mailing lists at a time, the costs could soon start to spiral. Having witnessed first hand how my 11 year old nephew spent a Sunday afternoon texting his girlfriend and other mates, as well as receiving his SMS updates from the Chelsea Football Club mailing list, it is quite scary how expensive this communication tool could become for the person picking up the bill!

You can't please all the people all of the time

With so many companies aiming to gain access to our email inboxes and rise above the noise of all the marketing messages that we receive electronically on a daily basis, it's no surprise that sometimes, some campaigns just fail to strike a chord with everyone they are targeted at. In a recent *New Media Age* article, for example, Salim Fadhley wrote that, as far as he was concerned, most viral marketing doesn't work.[24] The examples he gave included one campaign by PG Tips, created by Ogilvy Interactive,[25] where users were invited to download an application that reminded customers to take regular tea breaks. However, his claim for its being a 'horror' of a campaign was the fact that it required users first to download a large file, which had to be manually installed – a lot of trouble for something pretty unrewarding.[26] A second example that he gives is a viral campaign that was created to promote the release of the Spielberg movie *AI (Artificial Intelligence)*. In this instance, an extremely complex and highly original strategy had been put together with the objective of involving users in an addictive online game where those who had the time and inclination had to set about solving a murder mystery. The viral was initiated on the day the second teaser trailer for the film went live on the film's official website.

As described by the *Guardian*'s Paul Trueman, on that same day, someone calling himself 'ClaviusBase' emailed film journalist Harry Knowles at www.aintitcoolnews.com. The email pointed out that something very strange was going on with the trailer, something that had never been attempted before – the filmmakers had placed two coded messages at the end of it. ClaviusBase had noticed that on the credits at its end, Jeanine Salla is listed as 'Sentient Machine Therapist' alongside the usual names of producers and writers. 'Type her name in the Google.com search engine and see what sites pop up', Knowles was told in the email.[27]

Intrigued, I tried this for myself – damn, caught in the viral affect! – but only in the name of research. I will come back to what I found shortly, but at the time the viral was released, had you carried out the search on Google.com, as instructed, you would have come across Jeanine Salla's Home Page. From this website, if you hadn't got bored yet, you discover a totally fake world of other personal home pages, all connected somehow with each other, all set in the future and all forming part of the murder mystery game. However, as Trueman rightly pointed out in his article, not one of these many websites mentions the film *AI* or even acknowledges a world outside the 22nd century, other than to refer to 'the warning' that took place 100 of years earlier, drowning millions.[28]

Apparently thousands of people have now visited these website – and I'm one of those sucked into the hype! However, the reason I can sympathize with Fadhley's views is that, I find, more often than not, campaigns are created where the overriding objective appears to be one of winning industry awards for creativity, rather than achieving the original marketing objectives of the overall campaign.

While there is no doubting the ingenuity of this viral idea, I honestly do not know why its creators went to so much trouble. The campaign may well have generated a certain amount of PR coverage. However, I question whether or not it made the average cinemagoer, who is likely to be deciding on his or her bimonthly trip to the flicks, choose *AI* over another film, because of a cryptic mystery game played on the internet. I wait to be convinced.

Now back to what I discovered when making the search on Google.com seven months after the viral campaign was released. Third link down on the Google.com search results page was a link to a website on Geocities.com with the heading 'Jeanine Salla' and the following description:

"Jeanine Salla is alive and well. That *AI* movie isn't very good; it ranks about the same quality as Spielberg's *Always*: mediocre product from a good filmmaker...**"**

Oh dear. I rest my case!

KEY POINTS AND TOP TIPS

- Brands whose characteristics are of a comical, cheeky and humorous nature lend themselves to viral marketing campaigns.
- Tele-viral adverts are television-type advertisements produced solely for viewing on the internet.
- Online movies can be tagged to link to a web page to help drive traffic to a site.
- Comical content is well suited for viral distribution.
- Free offers can motivate people to forward emails.
- Be careful not merely to acquire those people who want a freebie if that is your campaign offering as they may have no interest in becoming a customer.
- Campaigns that include 'Forward to a friend' mechanisms via a website can maintain more control if managed by email servers running databases monitoring the send.
- Try to ensure users do not continue to be sent the same campaign too many times to avoid negativity of the brand due to high frequency intrusion of their inbox.
- Viral marketing campaigns do not have to link to a website to be successful if the objective is to generate or increase awareness of a brand or subject matter.
- Video messages from celebrities or industry icons can help to encourage users to pass on the message.
- SMS is a powerful tool for viral marketing to teenagers.
- Successful viral marketing campaigns do not involve the recipient to do too much work.

Take one joke, add naked girl and free trip and send for five minutes

Is viral marketing science or art? Is there really a magic formula for viral marketing success? Can it possibly be like one of Delia Smith's recipes whereby, if you use the right ingredients and follow her basic instructions, even the most undomesticated man can make beans on toast?

Is viral marketing science or art?

I'm afraid that if you were hoping this book would provide you with an all-encompassing step-by-step guide on how to create the perfect viral marketing campaign, you will be sadly disappointed. Unfortunately, I do not believe there is a Holy Grail of viral marketing, simply because there are too many variables involved when planning a campaign. Different things motivate different groups. There will be very little comparison between a campaign designed to encourage women to donate to charity and one encouraging men to vote for the sexiest women in the world. It's also impossible to know exactly how people are going to react at any given moment. With email, you are dealing with a live environment where anything can happen in between the time you send your message and the time it is forwarded to someone else. Who is to say that what you thought was a highly creative idea has not already been planned by your main competitors? And what if, when you start your viral campaign, you discover that those same competitors sent their campaigns out virally the night before? Your viral campaign ends up as a damp squib while your competitors' surge around the world, simply because consumers had had enough of 'splat the latest celebrity to fall from grace' for one week.

Having said all that, while I do not believe there *is* one all-encompassing formula for success, if we understand who our target audience is and what motivates them and turns them on, we can go some way to predicting what we believe they may do. In this chapter, I outline my thoughts on how to create a successful campaign. In the meantime, I certainly do not recommend that you go to the extreme lengths Nintendo and E4 did in the USA when they hired an ex-computer hacker who had been accused of breaking into US military computer systems to help develop a viral marketing campaign for them.[1] It can't be that much of a mystery, surely?

A number of US companies are taking this new form of marketing very seriously, however. In a study by IMT Strategies, conducted in 2001, they found that the vast majority of marketers were planning to launch a viral marketing campaign within the next 12 months, 97% of their survey, with 67% having already conducted one.[2] However, the same people felt that viral marketing was poorly understood and that there were real risks to implementing it. Further figures reveal that 26% of the respondents perceived viral marketing as 'more art than science' since it does not allow for a high level of control. They also felt that the key issues in gaining success included knowing how to trigger customer-to-customer advocacy, segmenting existing customers who are receptive to viral marketing and understanding the incentives for a campaign to succeed.[3]

The respondents to IMT Strategies' survey were also divided on whether promotional dollars were necessary to power a viral marketing campaign, with 48% saying it was and 48% believing it wasn't. It was a similar story when asked if they felt compelling animation was required to achieve the same aim, with 40% saying yes and 43% no, with 17% unsure.[4]

IMT Strategies also found that the size of the organization had a significant bearing on how experienced the company was with regard to viral marketing. The report states that smaller organizations will lead innovation and larger organizations will insist on positive demonstrations of how viral marketing will increase sales. Their findings showed that companies with incomes under $100 million were more likely to have experimented with viral marketing. They also outlined the fact that only 24% of companies showing revenues of over $500 million described viral marketing as 'very important' as compared to 43% of those with revenues under $10 million.[5]

So finally, here is a 20-point checklist on what to consider when setting about creating the perfect viral marketing campaign:

1. Plan your campaign.
2. Understand your audience – research them.
3. Is viral marketing appropriate in this instance?
4. Where can you find your audience?
5. What motivates the group?
6. Will you need an incentive and, if so, what should it be?
7. Have you checked all the legalities?
8. Who will own the campaign?

9. How will you seed the viral spread?

10. How will you measure success?

11. Are you set up to monitor the campaign?

12. Is the timing correct?

13. What restrictions are there on your delivery methods?

14. What geographical restrictions are there?

15. Should you use an attachment?

16. Do you need to drive traffic to a website?

17. How complicated is the campaign execution?

18. Who are your e-fluentials in the group?

19. What controls have you put in place?

20. Follow it up.

Viral marketing checklist

Plan your campaign

An old marketing adage goes something like: 'If you fail to plan you are planning to fail.' This is never more true in a viral marketing campaign. Some people believe that viral marketing is simple. That you can send one email to a few friends, and before you know it, you have created a world phenomenon. But there is far more to it than that. Planning is crucial in every aspect of the campaign and, in particular, in ensuring you are set up to deal with success that you will no doubt achieve – after all, there's no point going into a campaign if you do not think it will be successful. But depending on what your campaign objective is, there may be any number of things you have to ensure you are set up to handle. For instance, is your campaign going to drive significantly more traffic to your web-

Whatever your objective, expect success and plan for it.

site or a specific movie that you are streaming online? Is the campaign going to make the phone lines ring constantly with new enquiries? Whatever your objective, expect success and plan for it.

Understand your target audience – research them

One would expect to have a certain knowledge on your target audience given you will no doubt already be marketing to them. However, it's always appropriate to ensure you have fully understood their lifestyle habits. After all, if they do not use email or SMS, then viral marketing is not the route to go and you can stop at this point.

Is viral marketing appropriate in this instance?

Once you have identified your target audience, ensure that there is a need for viral marketing. If there is a finite number of people you are trying to reach and you know exactly who the individuals are, there may be a strong case to consider alternative methods of marketing to them.

Where can you find your audience?

Accepting that your target audience use email, SMS or both, you still need to know where you can find them. Do you already have a database of customers to start your campaign? If not, you need to find where these people are – what websites do they visit, what papers and magazines do they read, what radio stations do they listen to? This type of profiling will help when you come to seed the campaign.

What motivates the group?

How do you know what will motivate the group into passing on your message? When you have identified who the audience is and where you can find them, sometimes you may need to

do further research in understanding what these like-minded individuals are interested in, aside from your product or service, of course. Do they respond to comedy or good cause campaigns? Do they like to be challenged or do they simply like to win things?

Will you need an incentive and, if so, what should it be?

In establishing the motivating factors that will help you develop your creatives for the campaign, at some point you may need to make a decision on what kind of incentive you will provide, if appropriate. For example, should you give numerous gifts away for free? Some people may argue that certain companies may not want to give away freebies all the time as this act eats into their credibility and brand equity.

Have you checked all the legalities?

There is a whole host of legal checks that you may need to consider depending on the content of your campaign, and who it is aimed at. While there may be a large number of grey areas when it comes to viral marketing, it is still wise, for example, not to offend an individual or a sector of society such as a minority religion for example. Alternatively, will there be an outcry if your campaign landed in the inbox of a minor, when you are promoting, for example, an alcoholic brand?

Who will own the campaign?

When you have decided to embark on this campaign, make a decision on where the ownership will lie. If you are handling the campaign in-house, ensure you have the resources to deal with the tracking, the reporting, the response to enquiries generated, etc. If you are giving the brief to your marketing agency, then allow a number of agencies to pitch for it. It will be interesting to see the different responses you receive from your PR agency, advertising agency or New Media specialist and, of course, the variations on price quoted. Ask the questions of them in terms of how the campaign is being developed – are they using contractors or freelancers? Will you be getting the same developers that put together the wonderful examples of their work that they are bound to show you in their pitch documents? Who will manage the campaign for you? What experience do they have of viral marketing? Never be afraid to question why. And finally, do not allow your agency to pitch to you campaigns that may win industry awards for creativity, but have no chance of allowing the consumer to understand exactly what they are meant to do. As with other forms of advertising, you have a very limited time in which to catch someone's attention using a medium such as email. However, what email does bring is the ability for the user to forward the message instantly to a number of other people with a note saying something such as, 'look at this rubbish I just received'.

How will you seed the viral spread?

The answer to starting a viral marketing phenomenon is not to send it to a few friends and family and hope that will kick start thousands upon thousands of strands of messages. Viral marketing is not that simple – if it were, everyone would be doing it. Seeding the campaign, i.e. sending out the viral campaign to a select group of individuals to initiate the spread, needs to be very targeted. Again, it will depend on your product or service and the audience you are trying to reach when deciding how many people you need to seed the campaign with. Also, if your campaign is an application or a movie, it is possible to offer it to other websites as downloadable content for their users. Sometimes, certain sites may require an incentive to do this, whether for its editor or their users or simply an investment above the line. Either way, this is often a very effective route to

ensure your campaign is in front of the people you need to reach. The people who frequent these 'seeding points' are referred to by Justin Kirby of DMC as 'alphmailers', i.e. those people that proactively seek out viral-based material and pass it on, helping to kick start the viral spread.[6]

How will you measure success?

As with any marketing campaign, measuring success is very much dependent on the objectives you have set yourself and these will impact on the type of viral campaign you design anyway. For example, are you looking at driving click-through or simply seeking a specific number of people to view your brand or message? Will you consider a viral campaign a success on the basis that more people saw the campaign than it was originally sent to – hence it must have grown virally at some stage?

Are you set up to monitor the campaign?

There are several ways in which you can report on the success of the campaign. For example, if it's impressions on your site that you are hoping for, perhaps have the viral link to a specific URL that you can monitor on your traffic log reports. Alternatively, the viral may simply drive traffic to your home page. In this case, you may well see the log report show that the number of non-referral links to your site has increased, i.e. those that haven't come from another website but have either clicked on a link from an email or typed in your address directly to their browser.

There are clever ways of finding out if people are viewing a movie that you've sent out virally. For example, Justin Kirby of DMC embeds code in a .mov file so that the clip makes a call to his server if the user plays it when online. He also includes a hotspot in the movie that enables the user to click on it and

TAKE ONE JOKE ...

visit a website, so he can monitor when this is clicked too. His tracking system enables him to see how many times his movie is downloaded from his initially seeded sites and this also give him the user's IP number. He can then see the ratio of how many people subsequently saw it online and, where he includes a hotspot, how many people who click on formats like .wmv and .mov visit the destination page.

If the movie is then seen online by someone who wasn't one of the original people to download it, he can tell from their IP address, which tells him the viral agent has been passed on since the initial seeding point. Kirby then extrapolates the data to work out how many people also saw the campaign offline but were also not part of the group that initially down-loaded it.

Having tracked campaigns for about 12 months, Kirby suggests that between 60% to 70% of his viral material is being looked at offline.

After monitoring the activity for the .wmv and .mov files, which act almost as a control for the campaign, Kirby then issues the .mpeg version of his movie. He is then able to esti-mate the statistics of this second phase of the campaign based on his findings from the initial send.[7]

Obviously, if it's awareness you are looking to measure, then any tool that enables you to monitor how many people have seen your campaign like Kirby's one is still relevant. However, pre- and post-campaign awareness among a group of targeted online consumers can be carried out using traditional research methods that would work just as well for online too.

Is the timing correct?

Timing has an effect in terms of what time of day you send out an email, especially when you are sending it to either work-based or home-based email addresses. From my own experience of my company's office, Friday afternoon tends to be the time when the emails start pinging around the office. It's the time when the team is winding down for the weekend, the mood is good as the working week draws to a close and everyone is happy to receive non-work-related information – not saying *I* am happy for them to do so mind you! Catch them during the week when the pressure is on to complete a task for a campaign we're working on, however, or to complete a proposal and ensure it's through the door in time and you may find that you get a different response. If an email is received that is not relevant to them at that point, it may be deleted without even being read.

Similarly, in monitoring the responses to my survey on Tickbox.net, which tends to be Hotmail or personal email addresses rather than work-based ones, the majority of activity occurred at weekends or in the evening.

If it's an SMS campaign, again, timing is even more important as was shown in one of our case studies, when, if it is kids you are targeting, don't send the initial messages during school hours.

As well as time of day and week, the time of year is also something to consider. For example, Christmas is a notorious time of year for receiving viral marketing campaigns. Examples include applications that put Christmas lights on around your monitor's screen or a game of elf bowling. Whatever it is you are hoping to send out at this time of year, you can rest assured that lots of other companies have the same idea. These campaigns then become part of the noise along with the applications that are already out and about in cyberspace that seem to reappear every year. This reoccurrence seems to happen when someone is new to email during the year. He or she then believes that no one else must have seen the Christmas lights or elf bowling game as he or she hasn't. So they send it to all their friends, not knowing those friends, who have had email since 1994 have had to put up with this same routine every year – sorry, I drifted into a private rant for a moment!

What restrictions are there on your delivery methods?

Again, this is an issue in terms of understanding where your target audience is based and how they receive the messages. If they check emails from home, are they likely to be on a 56K modem, in which case, you certainly do not want to be attaching large files to an email that takes an age to download. If however, they connect to the internet from work, you may find there are different restrictions on what attachments they can receive there.

If you are streaming something from the web, have you considered how many concurrent users you are allowed to have at any one time viewing your film?

If it's an SMS campaign, remember that not all network providers support the same format of text messaging in terms of flashing characters, for example.

What geographical restrictions are there?

Viral marketing is extremely difficult if you are trying to localize a campaign. However, going international can cause just as many headaches. How frustrating for someone in the USA who's just as loyal to your brand, but receives something that means they can only enter the related competition if based in the UK. Alternatively, what if your intention is to be humorous or play on some form of innuendo whereby the result is that, in a different country or even region within the same

country, the message is not taken as a joke, but, instead, offends?

Should you use an attachment?

This is always a hotly disputed discussion topic. There are many people who argue the case not to attach files to any form of email campaign and I can understand and sympathize with this point of view. After all, there are a large number of users and companies who have been badly hurt by email viruses in the past. Often, these have been hidden within a .exe file and this has put them off both receiving and opening attachments of this kind, especially if it's something they were not expecting to receive. I, therefore, believe that you should shy away from attaching something to an email if it can be avoided, especially where development budgets are tight. Alternative solutions could be to embed files into an HTML email or link to a website within the email.

However, if budget is not an issue, then I would recommend continuing with both methods of delivery. As was shown in my survey findings in Chapter 3, there is still a large majority of users who *will* open such files, regardless. I believe that large numbers of viral marketing campaigns should accept that there might well be some wastage in terms of the audience reach. However, if the budget allows it, where the objective is to ensure that the greatest number of people in a target audience will see the campaign, you should always make all delivery options available.

Do you need to drive traffic to a website?

This is another objectives question but a very important one as this will have an impact on the type of campaign you create. Some of the highly successful television adverts that have been sent virally have not linked to websites. The objective was to ensure that the public saw the ad without the companies having to pay for media space on TV.

How complicated is the campaign execution?

Never has KISS ('Keep it Simple, Stupid') been more relevant than with viral marketing. It is very easy to forget that while the people designing the viral campaign may well use New Media technologies almost every minute of their working day, the people who the campaign is targeted to – more often than not the general public or business users – do not. These people will not necessarily know what a plug-in is, may think that Shockwave is something that occurs after a bomb has exploded, that Flash is a song by Queen or a floor cleaning product and that streams are wet places to go paddling in. The moment you ask users to do any additional work before they can interact with your campaign, you have lost them.

> **The moment you ask users to do any additional work before they can interact with your campaign, you have lost them.**

Who are your e-fluentials in the group?

This is a very tough task to solve. I specifically haven't said problem, as I do not believe that finding your e-fluentials is the be all and end all of a viral campaign. However, you can go a long way to helping yourself gain success if you can identify these individuals among your customer or client base who have stronger influences than most over their peers. If you have regular dialogue with a mailing list of customers or take feedback on your website, perhaps study some of the people who have been willing to contribute to discussion forums. Find out those who are willing to voice an opinion, but who, at the same, can also advocate your brand and products. If they are loyal to you, and you know you have something that

will excite them, they could be a great place to start to get feedback on your prospective campaign.

What controls have you put in place?

Is your campaign going to be a hit and hope or will you be prepared to test more than one creative idea? Any decent banner advertising campaign will run a number of creatives with each site that the campaign is booked with at the start. If, for example, the objective of the campaign is click-through, the planner buyer should monitor which creative is performing best on each site in terms of response rates and move all impressions that are still to be delivered to the better performing creatives. Likewise, with a viral send, if you have set up your measurement tools and are monitoring the success, ensure you have a control on the campaign to measure against if you want to try to change or adapt the campaign after launch. Obviously, once a viral message is out, you have to be careful not to have too many variations of the same theme as this may complicate matters.

Follow it up

I am amazed at the amount of times I have seen companies execute a campaign online and then do nothing to maximize its success. Your original objectives will influence how you follow up your campaign. The main thing is, however, that you do not let slip any inroads you have made to convince your target audience to interact with you. What if your goal is to have someone make a conscious decision to opt in to receive more information from you, having been recommended to visit your website because they received an email from a friend saying how wonderful you were as a company? If this is the case, you will do more damage by not following the enquiry up than you would have done by not starting your viral marketing campaign in the first place. If you commit to any form of marketing campaign, expect success. I view this as a typical half-empty half-full scenario. If you start a campaign expecting it to fail, then it will probably do so. If you go into it expecting success, then don't be surprised when that success occurs and ensure that you are ready to follow up on it so that you do not lose the momentum and lead you have built up on the rest who are not carrying out a similar strategy.

CHAPTER 6

Final words

I was asked to write this book because one of the Pearson Business publishing team had seen me present in front of a few hundred people on the subject of viral marketing at a New Media conference in London.

I have been working within the field of New Media marketing since 1994 and the reason I love what I do is that every day I am learning something new. There is always a fresh challenge to face and I work in an industry that is forever developing new technologies and channels to help me reach the target audiences of my clients.

We live and work in a world that is getting smaller by the hour in terms of being able to communicate with others. Every day there are people connecting themselves to the internet for the first time or buying a new mobile phone for themselves or their kids. Each time this happens, it means the case for viral marketing gets stronger as more people can be reached by either email or SMS. However, it also means more people sending more messages, which could potentially damage the concept to the point where it becomes as annoying as all the junk mail that comes through your front door every morning. However, the winners will be those who manage their campaigns to the point where the audience feel the emails or text messages received from friends, family and colleagues happen because those involved are sending them simply because it forms part of that desire to communicate with one another. As soon as it appears to be simply another 'me too' marketing campaign where one brand is copying the strategy of another, that's when we will start to struggle. What we don't want to end up with is campaign after campaign where the endorsement from the friend or colleague becomes transparent as that particular message becomes the tenth time in the same week that another friend wants your help to win a prize.

I hope that this book has given you food for thought and has helped you to understand a little more about the intricacies of viral marketing. It may have helped you in campaigns you are planning, tempted you to try a campaign or put you off forever. Whatever outcome has been generated from your reading it, please feel free to email me your viral marketing experiences. You can reach me at russell.goldsmith@markettiers4dc.com. And finally, if you do send me an email, it will be totally private – I promise *not* to forward it to anyone else.

Notes

Introduction

1 www.friendsreunited.co.uk
2 Article by Caspar van Vark: 'Longer term relationship'; *Revolution*, 29 August 2001, p. 21
3 'FriendsReunited grows to fend off challengers', *New Media Age*, 11 October 2001, p. 3
4 Article by Rachel Jackson: Start Up Profile, 'The best days of your life?', *e.businessreview*, October 2001, p. 20
5 Ibid

Chapter 1

1 Article by David Ferris: 'Catch it if you can'; *Streaming Media*, July/August 2001, p. 74
2 Interview by author with Dave Gorman: 8 October 2001
3 Ibid
4 Ibid
5 Ibid
6 Emanuel Rosen, 'The Anatomy of Buzz', promotional website: www.emanuel-rosen.com
7 Ibid
8 Report in 'Tactical Insights' by IMT Strategies, Stamford, 2001, CT, USA: 'Viral Marketing – A disciplined approach to using customers and prospects as a sales & marketing channel', www.imtstrategies.com
9 *Guardian Education*, 1 February 1994, p. 4, article by Peter Kington: 'Direct Action 94'

10 Interview by author with Justin Kirby for this book, Managing Director, Digital Media Communications, 21 February 2002
11 Supra, note 9
12 Ibid
13 http://www.drapervc.com/epress/epress factsfrset.html – article by Steve Jurvetson and Tim Draper: 'Viral Marketing'; original version published in the Netscape M-Files, 1997; edited version published in *Business 2.0*, November 1998
14 *Business Week*, 25 August 1997
15 Supra, note 13
16 Ibid
17 Ibid
18 Ibid

Chapter 2
1 Mobile Data Association as reported in *New Media Age* article by Clive Walker, 30 August 2001, p. 16
2 Ibid
3 'Unleash your ideavirus', Seth Godin from FC issue 37, p. 115
4 www.roperasw.com
5 Study by Burson Marstella and Ropar ASW, 'Efluentials key to online success', January 2002
6 Interview by author with Idil Cakim of Burson-Marstella: 27 February 2002
7 Forrester's UK Internet User Monitor 5 July 2000
8 Jupiter Media Metric, Viral Marketing overlooked by retailers; 25 July 2001
9 www.chinwag.com
10 http://news.bbc.co.uk/hi/english/uk politics/newsid 1604000/1604152.stm – 17 October 2001
11 Ibid
12 Ibid
13 Dr Ralph F Wilson, e-commerce consultant: 'The Six Simple Principles of Viral Marketing', *Web Marketing Today*, issue 70, 1 February 2000
14 Ibid
15 http://www.drapervc.com/epress/epress factsfrset.html – article by Steve Jurvetson and Tim Draper: 'Viral Marketing'; original version published in the Netscape M-Files, 1997; edited version published in *Business 2.0*, November 1998

16 Ibid

17 Prentice Hall Online Tutorial – Consumer Buying Behaviour

Chapter 3

  1 www.newmediazero.com: article by Brian Porter: 'Europe's teens are prime target for viral marketing'

  2 Ibid

  3 Interview with Sarah Boorman, Marketing Co-ordinator, Cartoon Network Interactive, 12 November 2001

  4 Ibid

  5 Ibid

  6 Ibid

  7 Ibid

  8 Ibid

  9 Ibid

10 NOP Family, Kids.net Survey, April 2001

11 *Director*, June 2001 – article by Nigel Coombs: 'The cheque is in the e-mail', p. 82

12 Silicon.com: Happy birthday: Email @ 30

13 *BBC Online*, article by Mark Ward: 'H@ppy Birthday to you', 8 October 2001

14 *Director*, article by Nigel Coombs: 'The cheque is the the e-mail', June 2001, pp. 81, 82

15 Ibid, p. 82

16 *E-Volve*, 29 March 2001

Chapter 4

  1 AdultShop.com – Viral Marketing Q & A, answers by Amanda Cooper, Head of Marketing

  2 AdultShop.com Press Release 'Big Boy Briefs – pump it up!', July 2001

  3 AdultShop.com PR material supplied by Sarah Sproule, Global Public Relations Manager, AdultShop.com 15 October 2001

  4 Ibid

  5 Article by Craig Liddell: 'Sex Creates Viral Marketing Success', Internet.com, 9 August 2001

  6 AdultShop.com PR material supplied by Sarah Sproule, Global Public Relations Manager, AdultShop.com 15 October 2001 and 1 November 2001

7 Ibid

8 Ibid

9 Article by David Murphey for *The Marketing Portal*, Chartered Institute of Marketing, 2000

10 Article by Matt Haig for *Guardian Unlimited*, 'Spread it by Word of Mouse', 15 February 2001

11 Virgin Wines Campaign email

12 Interview with David Godden, Head of Professional Services, e2 Communications Europe Limited, for this book, 25 October 2001

13 clevermedia.com

14 www.mindarrow.com

15 Ibid

16 Ibid

17 www.tmxinteractive.com

18 Flytxt case study presented by Carsten Boers at Flytxt London seminar 22 November 2001

19 Ibid

20 Ibid

21 Ibid

22 Ibid

23 Ibid

24 Article by Salim Fadhley: 'Non-Infectious Viruses', *New Media Age*, 7 August 2001

25 *New Media Age*, Ad Watch, 28 June 2001

26 Article by Salim Fadhley: 'Non-Infectious Viruses', *New Media Age*, 7 August 2001

27 Article by Paul Trueman: 'Kubrick's strange afterlife': *Guardian Unlimited*, 30 April 2001 – www.guardian.co.uk/Archive/Article/0,4273,4177669,00.html

28 Ibid

Chapter 5

1 *The Register*, article by John Leyden: 'Ex-hacker to help Nintendo with viral marketing', 29 March 2001

2 Report in *Tactical Insights* by IMT Strategies, Stamford, CT, USA: 'Viral Marketing – A disciplined approach to using customers and prospects as a sales & marketing channel' – www.imtstrategies.com

3 Ibid

4 Ibid

5 Ibid

6 Email follow up to 21 February 2002 interview by author with Justin Kirby for this book, Managing Director, Digital Media Communications, 8 March 2002

7 Ibid

More power to your
[business-mind]

Even at the end there's more we can learn. More that *we* can learn from your experience of this book, and more ways to add to *your* learning experience.

For who to read, what to know and where to go in the world of business, visit us at **business-minds.com**.

Here you can find out more about the people and ideas that can make you and your business more innovative and productive. Each month our e-newsletter, *Business-minds Express*, delivers an infusion of thought leadership, guru interviews, new business practice and reviews of key business resources directly to you. Subscribe for free at

● **www.business-minds.com/goto/newsletters**

Here you can also connect with ways of putting these ideas to work. Spreading knowledge is a great way to improve performance and enhance business relationships. If you found this book useful, then so might your colleagues or customers. If you would like to explore corporate purchases or custom editions personalised with your brand or message, then just get in touch at

● **www.business-minds.com/corporatesales**

We're also keen to learn from your experience of our business books – so tell us what you think of this book and what's on *your* business mind with an online reader report at business-minds.com. Together with our authors, we'd like to hear more from you and explore new ways to help make these ideas work at

● **www.business-minds.com/goto/feedback**

[www.business-minds.com
www.financialminds.com]